THE
LIGHT IN THE
DARKNESS

An Anthology of Thought-Provoking Poetry

'For a single moment I pause and reflect
.......then onwards my journey goes'

By Cliff Latimer

ISBN 978 0 86071 914 4

A Commissioned Publication Printed by

MOORLEYS
Print, Design & Publishing
info@moorleys.co.uk • www.moorleys.co.uk

The views, thoughts, and opinions expressed in this book belong solely to the author, and do not necessarily reflect the views of the publisher or any of its associates.

Contents

The Light in the Darkness

I'd walked my life in darkness insurgent beguiled.
Rampant for a money trail, I was vicious and so wild.
Never dared to look inside what developed, I'd become.
Doused out all my memories with drugs, Bacardi rum.

Gave little hint to love ties, outside there was more sport.
Daily thieving practices, until for sure your caught.
Devil may care my attitude, except deal out pain.
Life's lessons even prison, bars barter listen gain.

Then from gutter found by God, lifted to His sight.
I wandered yes unsure at first, but strode into His Light.
Felt lifted to existence a portrayal of differed man,
I asked so many questions He answered if I can.

He can't give you information, you must live and do your best,
no judgement's there before you, no written question test.
Give those boulder's heavy, lay at the foot of cross.
Let His grace enfold you, your mind in He emboss.

Sing His praises daily, be joyful friends delight.
A choir of Angel's there for you as you step into His Light.
© Cliff Latimer 2023

Frozen Moment

Stood still that day her face espied
To all I spoke, upset denied
No bother me at all she's dead
Yet again spins round my head
Proceed I can't, in time I'm froze
Writing poem, verse, and prose

The fears surround let someone near
The heartstrings pulled, alas, o dear
Yet a voice states now, let go do grieve
It's a complicated web, constructed, weave
One billion broken pieces glued
One thousand women love pursued

And yet when love is there so near
My hand to touch, is filled with fear
A space in mind I enter darken
Will I survive, my plea do harken
Aid me from this shattered grave
Give me life, rescue, save
I promise I'll be good, so kind
The man but once is left behind

My plea in self to feel anew
To state as man in life I grew
Please aid to enter realms so cruel
Tie carefully the thread to spool
Do bring me back to minds own space
Please give to me prior place

My hope aspires, my dreams come true
To feel such pride, to feel brand new
This feeling is for future fore
First, I must enter door
The terror swilling filled with dread
Just thoughts but once inside my head

02/08/1999

A Diamond

A Diamond Treasure, Priceless Stone,
This Lass Who Showed Me Care
Eyes' Of Blue Reflected
A Maiden Fair of Hair

Intellect Resounds in Voice
Her Words onto I Latch
The Man Who Steals This Beauty
Holds Such a Priceless Catch

I Look Bespelled Towards Her
My Heart Doth So Admire
Electric Current Flows Between
Like Buzzing Down One Wire

If Weighed In Carats
Rubies Sapphires Jewels or Pearl
No Amount of Gold Amassed
Could Outweigh Her Heart, This Girl
A Polo Driven Wisely
No Clean Or Oil Confess
Stories Of Her Part Unfold
In Trench coat With No Dress

Features Of an Angel
Body Of a Queen
If You've Missed This Lady
A Treasure Missed, Unseen

In Friendship We Have Blossomed
With Each One Heart So True
As Friends in This Location
I Send My Love to You

The Smell of Winter

Crispness in the air, a sneeze not of the bloom
Appetite depending steaks fat to now consume
Evergreens release their scent, hedge-rows feeling bare spikey thistles,
Fields so brown tread carefully, beware the shrill of birds now quiet,
hark carol singing choir the cackle of hewn wood to spit,

Place logs upon the fire in garden leaf mould rotting,
Aromas kitchen pour the squirrels scratching in search of hidden store
Winter coat brought forward, to atop that prior peg
On streets I hear the down and outs, a few coppers may I beg
Stockings filled with goodies, to touch upon to find these wonders
Sought in passing, when of course no eyes I'm blind

A Seeing

Snowflakes fall so many to Sally Ann astound
A billion, billion floating to make a blanket for the ground
Covered pure with whiteness, a sign all sin be done
The snow is followed by the light of one begotten son

So blessed our lives just could be if we to take his path
Or live in town Gomorra then God to face his wrath
Look with eyes of focus, the ones inside your heart
Turn leaf of life forgiveness, begin a brand-new start

Now blanket is of warmth, to wrap and keep within
Our lord he paid the highest price for we to hold no sin
Please look so deep inside yourselves, see if you be whole
Then pray with we so many for the peace of God made soul

Our church is one of blessing, we sing his praise to take
Then for one to look outside herself with a seeing of one snowflake

One Soul

Follow I to unknown realms of mind
The Id ensued, this ego blind.
Come do not fear, it is but self
We search for horror, crime and stealth.
Let's wander through those portals dark,
A whisper, sssh, keep quiet - hark!

Allowed I have for you to see
Those inner depths of solely me.
We've seen the terror walls cascaded,
Of wounds and hurt the scars once based.
The memories we've travelled far
To dove the galaxy, nearest star.

And see the pools, those ripples -life,
Three children dance, one man, one wife.
You calm the wordage, curt, so cruel.
The names once called - a dunce, a fool.
We stroll amid the inner soul -
Heartache, death turned cold as coal.

We travel further, nearer centre core,
You wish to face, now come, be sure.
Ah so we sly abroad due south,
You cannot sense my word of mouth.
None can line realms of these,
So private thought, I ask you, leave.

April 2001

Have You

Have you ever wondered
What folk would do if they didn't put others down
If they didn't snigger at mishaps small or if a person looked a clown
Have you seen in folk embarrassment when people stand and stare
Have you witnessed unkind words to boot do any really care

Have you noticed folk's expressions when you walk into a bar
Laughed loudly uncontrollable when you're stuck in burning car
Have you pure Christian thoughts and pose their angelic to the core
Then off t' pub for pious days and the hatred spiel doth pour

Have you ever watched them church folk
Who pray for peace mankind
They titter at your mishaps and chuckle backs behind
But if in the boots ont' toother foot
Cor blimey hear them bloomin' swear
They hunt around when it's one of own pray lord my kin to spare

Whose Mate

Different folk live upon this lance called earth
Only some can hold their hearts to show how much they're worth
None can see the future who they'll meet upon life's path
True friends can iron out their prides and have a guttural laugh
Honesty of hearths to hands here my friends are each
Only you can tell a story wise to give advice and teach

Mates you'll find are few and far but you can count on me
Always mate a phone call hence I'll be there just for thee
Sometimes I might stumble but my friends I'll kneel to pray
That you're wished many returns to date,
and a wish on your birthday

Universes

Beyond all reason and doubt there's a scared shrine to all
If we could travel threads of light where a person's large or small
If we could live upon a speck or do, we this unknown
If our voices travelled multitudes, we could hear a whisper moan

If our capabilities could match the stars
With unbridled powers within
We could float on moonbeams give to all,
Would this be classed as sin
Beyond and far beyond we can see but never touch
It's out of reach or out of time just a little ways too much

We are stuck with what were given
So make the most of what we've got
The world is shrinking far too quick to turn to drunken sot
If time stood still, we could introduce all structures bold or vague
We could mend create or build anew
We could rid the world of plague

If we could survive the holocaust of our bodies turned to light
It would heal all and everything we could put all wrongs right
But these dreams are just a pause
For the tiger predator of this world is of course primeval man

Magpies

A continuum of time, Meeting people moments ago
Pedals on the house to make it go
Arguing for supremacy
For girls for boys and master of all the domain

Lilybeth

One can sense a certain sparkle a glint in those blue eyes
A knowing look to uncle dear of the wherefores and the whys
Ten months but lived a lifetime in an instant she will know
In mother's arms two hearts as one this age for her to grow

Each share those treasured moments of a mother daughter bond
As age develops wisdom these memories dear so fond
A mother works behind a bar but cheery all is sensed
Two auras fold into one form the distances emensed

When saddened times approacheth those tears to fall as rain
The sights forth coming future wearing white a bridal train
A poem wrote upon a page a source of raw emotion
A gift this lass of Becky stance and praise for her devotion

Intensions

They visit with intensions to assess your structures needs
They ask before and after the questions are to leads
They come with tools enabling to ease thy daily chore
They exercise one's bodily girth to strengthen and much more

They listen to your tales of what to analyse agree
They rearrange one's thoughts arrange to put one's heart a plea
They manipulate and stretch one's bones to give a muscle tone
They're not hurtful in their exercise no pill until one moans

The Man I Am

I had to be who I was to become the man I am
No more a crook a thief no more looking for the scam

Pedals

Paying in shares in the house one percent one thousandth
Coins into purses bringing back the correct ownership

Nothing 2 Declare

I used to be a villain yeah do the bizz and cut the crime
If nicked if hold me 'ands up high sit ont pot an do me time
I used to so many things from tooting on a pipe
Use violence to the living world and anything to swipe
I'd use that billy whizz an stuff owt to get a high
Booze day and night to use more phet an never once asked why

I'd stay away from home for days an wondered why she left
Stole thousands in their hundreds but always nowt bereft
Id drink a cocktail pills and booze mulled an slowly spiced
I hungered with an empty soul and looked above my Christ
He called into my wilderness he raised the pain so raw
He walked around a mind so hard and made emotions purt

He led me to a pathway I listened to his voice
He smiled and said free will my son from now it is your choice
I live my life for Sundays to sing and praise so high
I walk a garden Eden inside
I might not know am doin wrong an maybe unaware
I'll stand in church on Sunday morn an state nuffin to declare

Journeys

I met a man upon the road they call the path of life
He stated love instead of hate not brutal club or knife
He spoke of feelings deep inside we hide from kin and kind
We strolled thus lane he smiled and strode a matter of my mind

We ambled down one street abound to conquer all my fears
In the dark times laid ahead in his spirit so appears
We circled round a cul-de-sac a portrayal of all my worth
He stroked my troubled brow,
or thought hence gave my place on earth

We ambled down an avenue tree lined so filled with green
He enquired where's thou heart my son fragmented hurt unseen
We marched around parade grounds where once a troubled youth
He showed me images frame by frame a villain their uncouth

We rode a highway bright and clear a place where one could pray
To bring one's troubles cares and woes when minds are in dismay
We toddled down a tunnel I fought to gain control
He smiled at me this man I'd met as he held in hands my soul
We have a little tipple in wisdoms of our youth
Don't what the outcome is the dancers on the proof

Life's Graces

Could one instantly just imagine distant lighting
through sightless eyes
Could one see through darkened portals
the lies through one's disguise

Could one feel the furrows of a race and know
the kindness there
Could you hold a child through harshest times
console her through despair

Would you build a bridge of fortitude
combining human strength
Would you save from burning building
the fifth or seventh tenth

Would you know the way to kingdom really,
blinded deaf and dumb
Most folk would turn in street
if spied helpful only some

No legs or arms just teeth to paint
but masterpiece displayed
Differed talents differed folk
from south to northern plaid

We could if only understood
the minds of other folk
To be disabled lacking health
disheartening to some a joke

In future times you'll see despair
discomfort give a care
This planet's soil for one
and each and heavenly bliss prepare

Inspired

I had this Christian skin design tattooed upon by back
I heard a thousand sermons stating nothing would I lack
I walked a path of righteousness as simply as I could
I thought about the past I'd held the soaking of thing blood

I wondered when I hungered these pangs went round my 'ed
I heard a whisper softly about sum fishes and sum bread
I knelt to pray of many times when doubt reached down inside
I spoke untruths to self and all but nowhere could I hide

I opened up my heart to all, and sometimes it got broke
I witnesses two unlikely gents who liked the way I spoke
I asked my lord forgiveness he answered this was don't
I realised the question a father gave his son

I ask my Christ to guide this wait to follow when he needs
I go to lengths of human gait and try to do good deeds
I look above and question why when things seem all uphill
I look unto his sacrifice and again I do His will

I write your worth in woodlands in glades and lowly glen
I state my love for saviour Lord and proudly close Amen
Saturday 16th August

Guilt

The shadows past comes into mind in dreams, a nightmare scare
The running racing intention the asking who goes there
Time and place one knows the truth but bickers should an cigs
Then future time in sleep state it bites you back surprise

One focuses on depth of dirt and sees the colour
One ponders why and when it went, yet its only down
Apologises are never too late what healing this will bring
One's spirit soars to heights unknown,
the church bells clap and ring

But doubt creeps in what, only, in, or don't accept my plight
Yet then again one sleeves in mind, another nightmare fright
Get up go out and meditate the reasons that thou must
A certain pride will come to pass
in oneself you've earned your trust

So ruminate through past vent ponder pause reflect
Then smile in sense of sweet success and one carries great respect

Sleep Patterns

I awoke yet again after another journey yarned through tiredness and yet
at peace, mashing my cup of tea I perused my thoughts where had I been
this time the past present or future in my dreams it didn't seem to matter
I'd always been able to drift out of my solid form to travel on a golden
thread always attached to my supernatural being

Heading over oceans roaring to sun drenched paradises or as small as
insects seeing the universe through smaller eyes wandering around a
redwood at a snail's pace circumnavigating the fine detail of its trunk then
heading to the heights of the tree's foliage the experience of such
adventures are exhilarating

Just imagine floating on a whisper of sound seeing different views in
different dimensions soaring high on a plume of smoke forging the chain
of life becoming an atom may their dreams come to fruition may their
hopes become reality and may their love conquer all endeavours

Fate

We don't know what's round the corner lying there in wait
Get knocked down or trampled one destiny of fate
Smoking could be hazardous choking up one's lungs
A thatcher doing roof work clambering down some rungs
Drinking now there's a no, no intoxifying brain
Don't the blood good either blue devils drove insane

Oil from underneath the ground must be drilled for final plume
Last breath is for the Chaplin a priest may one assume
A ganger on the road works danger lurks around
Digging chopping hewing all things underground
Me mum she'd say out Clifford av u changed your pants today
Cos a barton bus cud knock u down cor blimey they would say
There's one thing in the larder death and tazes for sure
Our destination final is what the lord has got in store

Enter

Enter all you tutors try to train this angry mind
The flogging never worked you see from the man and human kind
Enter in and sow your seeds in there let me witness all that's wise
Let me look into a human form through the portals of his eyes

Enter grow your plants galore open pathways for the light
Push through that passage hated let go of all that might
Enter open doorways long ago were shuttered locked
Sick and tired this spiteful soul jealous and always mocked

Enter free the fires in there or quell the searing flame
Scorch out every memory or all that hurt my name
Enter stride the chaos put there by simple men
Ease all the horrors of a child the sharpness of a pen

Enter close the doors tight shut don't let any in behind
Take all the hurt out with you put there by human kind
Enter through another entrance my ears to learn and know
Give your saplings many strengths
in mind so one day I'll surely grow

Kingdom

You won't be able to believe one's eyes
at such structure such expanse
It would take a billion lifetimes
to take it in at just one glance

The clarits the marvels of up to now unknown
You've died and gone to heavens realm
which would mean that you have grown

Grown into a spirit form with endless places reach
Kneel to your master God your faith in him do beseech
The light is bluish tinted some but brighter than a star
You can see your presence past and future know who you are

You've walked a path set out for you
from the beginning of your birth
He strode beside your presence all existence time on earth
But now you run with Father Lord play games upon a plain

And view mistakes but never to much the clouds form let it rain
Your joy in heart you'll always feel kneel to Lord and pray
He's watching waiting for it is child last gasp it is your day

He Knows

He knows our final outcome since the moment of our birth
He knows in all abundance the grains of sand on earth
He knows our final destiny but always its our choice
All we have to do is harken to his peaceful tones of voice

He knows the far flung galaxies from the moment they did form
He knew the distance to our world enuf to keep us warm
He knows our needs and wants in life but let's leave it in his hands
He knows of all complexity in truth he understands

We tread a path laid out for us but there again out choice
We can listen to the imps therein or a soothing gentle voice
He know of all decisions in life at length must make
And all the treacherous footsteps the first one we must take

If you wish to see the father then turn yourself from sin
And knock upon the door of life then enter let him in

Eternally

I can't get me ed around it how does one fit into there
There's Father Son and Holy Ghost cor it baffles me
But there again look at its size billions of light years
Every dread on words one's spoke a multitude of fears

Out sun its mass enormous I think its ninety three
Millions upon millions worlds the naked eye can see
A rainbow forms and likens to the spectrum of the sun
Rockets hurl towards far globes faster than a bullet from a gun

Beyond our massive universe lies others beyond our reach
But scientists and others known will stand on pulpit preach
If one black hole can hold our sun up to one million times
I cannot fathom all our sea's but put it hence to rhyme

Heaves gate a portal to a world among all worlds
The Milky Way andromeda one day destruction collide
He's stated that by fire this time already had the flood
Our sins forgave upon the cross by the shedding of saviour blood

We cannot think gigantic his playground for his brode
Then harken the angels choir do swear and cuss so crude
We'll see the lord in spending light a vision oh so true
Money gold and precious things a camel can pass through

My Lord I marvel at your being and your eternal light
I only hope I have wisdom strong to deceiver o'er your might

Silence

A flash of hands denotes a word but only hush is ever heard
A sense denied to only some a lifelong struggle to overcome
We mouth our words so one can read a passage
spelt to then succeed

I watch in awe as letters told a verse or story to unfold
A loss of sense from grace of birth to tell battles of their worth
In later years if deafness binds another sense rekindles finds
We chatter on a rapid speed but so behold one cannot read

A slower pave a gentle rap upon a table angry tap
I dread to think in all my fears the loss of sight or silent ears
With broken bones in time we'll heal slower lips I do appeal
In traffic zones my eyes a sense my feelings there to recompense

The sense of touch more magnified a gentle stroke to me applied
When weary so ill close my eyes wake up morn in glee surprise
The hustle bustle of shopping crowd the constant chatter isn't loud
But harked hear my only pleas to take ones time so I may see

Enrage

Do you want to see a demon etched upon this face
To snarl in verment speeches to put you in your place
If you tempt the sleeping energy which boils just below
Then prod and see him rise to hate feel the grimaced flow

A devil demon in the mind and body soon engulf
A life snuffed out in seconds a snarling snapping wolf
Don't press the buttons danger lurks cold a heartless stone
Its lived beneath for ever more its venom there to hone

Don't awaken sleeping evil cos ten is not enough
Tossed around like jackals prey a swipe just off the cuff
Don't whisper taunts of pledges don't date for him come hence
For the portal you've so opened just burning no pretence

Now go away and leave me be let me tarry be at peace
No demon woke today amen let's hope the hate will cease

Anger

It really pissed me off today I could have screamed a dicky fit
Why couldn't they have said something the stupid little git
I'm seething yeah I've lost control me head is in a mess
I don't know who to talk to if I killed do I confess

I think that everyone's involved a plot to do me in
What have I done wrong I'm good and without sin
I know I lose my temper but so do all the rest
I think my Lord almighty is putting me to a test

I could stamp my feet in anger blood boiling to the core
A castigating molten lava from internal does it pour
No answers are in rage I know but don't it make you sick
The medical Gordon government I think they think we're thick

Calm down I must be pleasant smile yet that's for sure
And I must be grateful I awoke took breath
and put my feet on the floor

Twins

We see ourselves as mortals and yet our spirits soars
Remote supply existence create mind games which so lures
Without the darkness thus within how can we distinguish lights
The battle of our inner selves the constant chatter fight

the mind universe their untold none can enter in
We tell the dog on ending and yet regard as sin
Two sides reside within this sphere the devil and saint say name
When darkness dwells I wear this dance, the stain is there so faint

The light brings wonders tenderness love a total goal
It reaches depths unknown to man to touch onst Berry soul
it shines around out or is the ones we all display
But let the dark there rain unchecked and all you'll find decay

Our rooms could be so different to shine upon this globe
then sends the petal of a flower on to kiss and a lobe
The lights of God and angels wise be sure to set him free then recognise
his portals set to journey you and me

Let Go

Let go of all that heat inside in the end it will destroy
With anger grows resentment than to hide yourself so coy
Manipulating feeling holding on to envy greed
All you're doing is decaying trust and you're in a demon feed

Fine no I said new line
Your mind is in a turmoil sickening to one score no
Let go the hurt so long ago let your heart beat there so pure
the things of past are gone no more, leave them on this shelf
Else deep within the venom looks and feels one's mind with stealth

Give your burden burdens freely lay them to our Lord
You feel so free in an instant your life has feigned reward
A lighter load means your forgive the hatred of your past
you'll see your path more clearly your joy will sell out last

Give sorrows and resentments lay them near the cross
Or forever feel the guilt of loss upon your mind emboss
30/07/21 4:50 AM

My Soul

I hope that I have proved myself from all my mortal sin
I've tried to redeem my deeds but where do I begin
A troubled way I do suppose but that I cannot blame
A mockery in youthful years many times I died of shame

I've begged forgiveness for my crimes when evil guided self
A fox a wolf in hiding my heart not pure but stealth
I cannot take my soul outside it's hidden from the horde
I did what I thought necessary and of my own accord

I hope and pray I've done enough to cleanse my mortal being
The truth will shine upon my death belief of thing there seeing
My Lord and Christ and Holy Ghost I implore to you be just
I've always felt someone was there just had to open up and trust

My soul I've tried with works thus hence boat works do not control
The light which shineth in one self the light which makes one whole

Dread

Fear can change your being to cower pain wracked face
To run away humiliated hide don't show disgrace
Put on a mask disguise the dread let hate fuel all contempt
Then visualise your future path all the precious things one dreamt

Let ruse become your standard fly the flag mistrust
Form heart one's heart unbreakable form a granite crust
Don't be forlorn and weak of mind gait your snarling teeth
Then let the darkness deep inside set free which lies beneath

You'll witness gore unending don't listen to them wail
Strike fast and lethal sword transfixed behead or so impale
If weakness enters in this realm the battles are but lost
Then you'll utter your penance, Oh dear my, my such cost

The prayers you'll pray forgiving as one lays upon a bed
All the sites of past you'll see and it started with just dread

The Vow

I vowed I would not be like him when married and had kids
I would not hit my wife or child in mind an oath forbids
I vowed that I would always love and cherish them from the start
In later years disaster struck and all Sunday to an apart

I fed them and so nourished ne'er what I had to do
I told them loving stories goodnight my heart be true
they were never sent to Coventry no one could speak a word
shouldn't from all my family ties was I guilty how absurd

Kicked and punched from my early age
one gets used to hurt and pain
Run away or many a time to find a different plain
hunger racked my stomach get used to it for years
no one heard my cries of pain no one saw my tears

A waif and stray a troubled kid who knew no better then
I look back now to punishment a glance at way back when
I did not hurt the ones I loved a promise I made to I
I honour this to dying day last breath there but one sigh

The Cross

He hung up on the cross of shame to end the sin of man
Endured the people's ridicule to see think finished plan
He bled for all eternity to gift his treasured blood
He smiled unto a nation cold some bowed and understood

He pleaded with his father forgive for what they do
A wish in death upon the cross that hearts would give so true
He had a sword thrust in his side to end the coil of life
A crown of thorns upon his head piercing like a knife

The nails upon his hands and feet no one could bear such pain
The heavens blackened with his cries thundered heavy rain
His blood was washed up on the soil at cavalry brought to bear
He asked forgiveness for his flock made a promise oath to swear

The mighty cross so cruel unkind yet a thrown my master bore
The message rang to far and wide the Messiah was the cure
I look upon the cross of pain I see my Lord of Lords
I answer to a king of kings and receive my just rewards

Our Choice

We choose our daily habits from drink or drugs or smoke
We burn our paper monies and all we do is choke
A decision made five weeks ago to quit the stench of cigs
But appetite increases so eat healthy fruits and figs

We know the rules a hard one to break the dreaded curse
But look to the future yonder tears of kin one hearse
My first cigarette at 7 my lungs on fire turned green
I wish my will had conquered a fag I'd never seen

The damage in my later life I cannot all undo
But breathe a breath not choking a quitter yes it's true
My cash I have in plenty now to buy goodies I can afford
But Kairen she's an angel we talk I ne'er get bored

She showed me path commitment to start this chosen course
The journey yes a distant path but at least you'll feel your life force
The mind is stronger than you think take it by the horn
Then breathe again my friends in tow for our lungs have been reborn

True Meaning

Train tag little monkey boy belittle bash and bruise
Maybe in one thousand hence some person they may use
Chide him beat him starve as well do not speak or let him utter
Some have sausage mash for tea but feed him bread and butter

Apply those hands to numerous tasks then tell him there no good
You've not that thing my lad or planed that piece of wood
Tell me how's your reading come on give smirk
Come on the moronic monkey boy you're a joke a stupid berk

Where's your head boy in your hands you daydreaming little prat
Weave a basket sew mail bags use hessian welcome mat
You've found these bars for taking drugs for drinking all that beer
Now as a child once that you were I'll thrash again sincere

Why do you take the home with me
don't you know I'm on your side
But speak through what do I mean it's just something I implied
Don't run away and hide again do not fill your heart with fear
Because I am for you my love deceitful hard sincere

Useless

Once told so many times through life
of the ways that they must change
These cumbersome inapt in traits one must emulate or rearrange
One's thoughts can be tempered can be forged into one's will
As the voice of one's obeyance looms one must alter burn instil

One must grant to one a process robotic in one's force
This keeps the motion of one's mind
which can be altered in due course
One can scream into one's empty void when no one's there to listen
You can see the threats of human form
as a spider's web doth glisten

One can find in life a merriment but only at one's wish
Keep calm work hard and do not see the spark inside of anguish
One must endeavour forge along ones truth of self installed
And yet this feeling, feeling dread as in a cage one's walled

One can hear it way before in the echoes of the sense
One can hear it in the hush before one can hear it in the silence

The Race

Do not try to conquer all your ails give to here on high
We are just mortal beings who in us all can do but try
He asks us for our sorrows our burdens upon our back
They weigh us down like mountain stones is placed within a sack

We race around trying to do all manner night and day
And in our haste we drift to sleep and then forget to pray
We live in times technology another burden to our cause
We race around like headless binds and never take a pause

We forget the he forged a universe that's puns to unknown reaches
In peace my son he gently states slowed down in mind he teaches
We live three score and ten or more until our time demise
But will we be a stubborn fool or in he be there and wise

We pass this plain but once in time then live in peace about
We're surrounded by a glorious light
and of course, love we're crowned in
So down reign in thy spirit rush heed his flight one bird
The new your day of reckoning to the king of glory laird

In Mind

I've lived my life in shadows to all to one to I
I've left my life deceitful phones and never one I questioned why
I've loved and laughed with everyone in pubs and bars throughout
I've stood to fight those bully boys just to slap or punch one clout

I've formed a skin like rhino to shield me from pretence
I've dreamed a world utopian but far reaching or past tense
I've lived in darkness black as coal installed in daily life
I've lived as father husband kind but hated handled knife

I've worshipped to a God unknown got bored and walked away
I've worked with people who prettify if challenged I no nay
I've watched all persons in my realm and I have stood aloof
I've smiled when all have let me down in this to I is proof

I hid from those who loved me
I've denied contact from human kind
But the terrors fears and all quashed dreams
were the shadows of my mind

Our Journey

The gossips tonight is lashing fierce
Whose integrity can we pierce
Honesty is undermined
Just devilment for humankind
Wicked rumours pour them out
She's a hussy he is lout

Condemn and judge your mote
Don't take live is fear your pride forsake
Decency and honour proud
To one's Lord shout out loud
The secret corner whisper hence
She's not worthy, words pretence

Assumption is for idle hands
Take hot irons torture brands
Let none escape the fleeing hoard
Let's make up lies no laying bored
Capture more as normal realm
Put your conquest to the helm

Abandon hope let despair reign
Justify such hurt such pain
Carry forth to one's accord
Ask forgiveness from precious Lord
Ask him in to enter realm
Put king of kings to one's own helm

Establish worth and loyal pride
Respect for all and non denied
Shout to the heavens fell the buzz
Forsake him not my Lord my Jesus

Bits and Bobs

My life is looked at in bits and bobs just a little at a time
When thoughts appear within my sight I put those down to rhyme
I sense the ending may been near so I cleanse my final role
The purity that I now see is the cleansing of my soul

I've tried in years just past and present for my crimes to so atone
I've walked a walk and talked a talk and done this on my own
I've peeled the onion looked in depth the hurt and so much more
I've delved within the realms of life to the centre very core

I've asked forgiveness for my lies and darker crimes unknown
I've stripped away my feelings bad, right to the very bone
I'd wish that I had other lives a King or Prince who knows
Then just a self pityness the life I lead bid flows
And in truth I denied my faith my being or family tree
Then now I would not write or I and I never was but me

Hope

Insults flow much easier than the civil tones of voice
Belittlement and undermine is of course each person choice
Reasoning daily hatred or what only feels for self
Endeavouring as always to fill ones heart with stealth

But wouldn't it be so nice to pay instead of punch
To have a conversation over tea and cakes or lunch
To give and share ones wisdom without a cheating smile
To listen to the sobbing pain, I'm not busy for awhile

If we gave but just an instant a moment of our time
We could change this world forever take out the filth and grime
We could aid each person's progress to challenge every day
We could state with honest heartfelt joy that we intend to stay

We could rid the plant of disease gambling drugs and dope
We could master what's inside ourselves
and give our world true hope

Masks

Forced entry into citadel prise open all my masks
Do not fail to question why my son no need polite to ask
Then welcome you've surmounted to entre chamber one
Can you see the errors in my ways I'm dying day be done

Go enter mask of uno in your guise I will allow
Do not plead with my forthcoming do not seek to entre brow
Praise now in thrice tomorrow and hence it is today
Do you want my focussed open I'm a sprits its time to play

Come entre sit my table the chair a thought in mind
Tell I seek in your sub conscious tell have you entre than to bind
Way I cannot be so open I really know myself
Deceit and con to I within furtive full of stealth
No go you will not enter beyond the realms of four
You see masks I have in thousands their hiding human core

The Pack

Staffies are aggressive, Bull Mastiffs are the same
Hunting dogs to scour the land in search of any game
Alsatians are the guard dogs to protect from outside force
Collies heard the sheep of land to put them on their course
Corgi's corral the equine race to chivvy in style
Greyhounds race their hearts out to catch the hare the prefect mile

Jack Russell's firk out rabbit holes to panic live in fear
Pekingese they are lap dogs to hold and pet so much
But beware that one day looming they'll snap just at ones touch
Put in a pack they change their route to threaten snarl and gnaw
They'll leave remains not many just lying on the floor

Highbury

A rouge I was a villain a prowler dark of night
A drunken sot using drugs always ready for the fight
Fires I made a plenty burnt fields and haystacks high
Never guilty of my crimes never questioned why

I'd steal the golden objects from jewellers and much more
A con man with a heart of stone and always knew the score
Then later life some folk came close asked me to disclose
I thought awhile and listened suggestions I suppose

At Highbury Hosp a sections to delve into my past
A diagnostic treatment to why my life outcast
Alwda was my first psych who asked me of my life
Why hatred bore my very soul to carry gun or knife

She advised a meeting with Jackie to assess
My total being mentally my life a bloomin mess
She took me under wing to guide these words which set me free
I've suffered from a syndrome Asperger's and ADHD

Hear Our Plea

My Lord I ask forgiveness for the many crimes I've done
I know as I was baptised my battle was all but won
I need to see your light lord within and outer plains
I see you all around us in snows in light in rains

You keep out planet spinning for gravity to take
You watched in your creation the mountains you did so make
Were grains of sand upon a sphere not worthy of your grace
Then all you have to deal with our heavens outer space

You built an entire universe from nothing but pure dust
Envisaged where the planets lay and so you formed a crust
You staggered planters from a burning star to protect life on earth
Then cooled and rain drops falling you plan had come to worth

We thank you for your patience to see our daily sin
To know when we'll perform that crime for you
can always see within
We act upon compulsions and see it is our choice
But let us harken closely and definitely hear your voice

An Army Built

He knows when were attacked within from smokin drink or drugs
He does not frown for our mistakes a gentle whisper hugs
He sees when we condemn ourselves and hide away from he
No need to cower in that corner all he wants to set you free

He looks upon his children and knows we all have choice
Then listen to the rustling wind this be one of voice
We pray that peace will reign on earth with u to lead our path
Then see the lines go up or down as the scale upon a graph

We know we have a purpose one only showed to we
We must bow up to our majesty open eyes so we may see
Give credence to our tasks in store do not let our deeds put down
To see the multitude held in faith no sea of doubt or frown

My father master spirit you've been there all the time
You brought us through the beatings the grossness of the slime
Let we stand as your army like a magician saying wallah
Dedication of the poem the mighty men of valour

Space

To walk upon this plain called life is a burden that's 4 sure
An yet they seek the answer a label fact or cure
They know nothing of the wisdom that's at their fingertips
All they know condemnation torture pain an whips

Yet youth can c the future present in the now
One can produce a plain of conscience but they rumble don't know how
An yet a human walks this dirt an sees all that's there
But walks upon a cloud of sense a cauldron but of where

Just believe in wot u c of girth a fact a word of life
Check in a road an travel feel pain its just strife
But look upon the dimensions a speck a dot unknown
Then u'll c a universe 4 all as a human there 2 hone

Natural Causes

You're going on the tick of time you're gone before the tock
Waiting patient winding down the force of one life's clock
They say we disappear no more in human form
But in spirit when your dancing free you can sure kick up a storm

They say that passing over is a painful fear affair
But one second is a span of life one final breath your there
They say that mortals never see their loved ones in demise
Then how can they communicate to ourself do we tell lies

They say no-one as ne'er come back through other plains to praise
And yet just like our Cilla says I'm back surprise, surprise
So no more doubting Thomas no more moppey rocks
It's time to party with the dead so you'd better pull up socks

The mortal is quite simple you never leave to die
But after life questions asked are usually but why

My Friend

A friend who listens lovingly no judgement there to scorn
She tells her part of life once lived the place where she was born
Openly we talk for hours of indiscretions of our past
But also look at directions took and a voyage long surpassed

The universe which we create the spirals of one turn
To wish upon a star once more unravelling to churn
Memories in nutshell forms enormous such expanse
And yet with vision memories sought we see the with one glance

Our paths have differed in time and grace persons of one field
Emotions still inside ourselves as yet to give to yield
We'll carry on our convos to dally take our time
And maybe as we are as friends I may put it thus to rhyme

I say I love you but no control just peace within my heart
One wish from both I suppose at will we've got a brand new start

My Child

I thank my son for loving me and the courage to say I'm wrong
To state that I'm important to my family firm but strong
He's mature in years of forties but expands in Christ his Lord
When he opens up his heart none around are bored

He brightens daily living but hasn't had it smooth
A youngster and a hard man but nothing he had to prove
He's gentle in his stature although he's six foot two
His belief is Jesus who certainly is so pure

My son strides with the Lord in tow and speaks his mind to all
His footsteps they are steadfast never skid or fall
He praises Lord Almighty for the gifts he has received
He knows the Lord's intensions insight he has perceived

He told me off just lately about my drinking out of hand
To stop is my own torture but I have to understand
He'll help in prayer as always my son my mentor strong
So in human terms I have it all how can I ever go wrong

Our Deb

My little bit of silva a precious diamond stone
We talk in depth of varied things and sometimes have a groan
She runs me round wherever nowts to trouble her
I'll say a trek to certain place her quote is when or where

A massage we have fortnightly Amanda is our host
We talk of things that's spiritual cor blimey seen a ghost
Our Deb knows how frustrated I get with daily chores
And sometimes I do rant and rave my feelings tense so pours

Our Deb has always got a smile for to brighten up my day
We wander here and there we do whatever comes our way
She sorts out probs of white goods a freezer cooker all
And tells me all the details no matter how minor small

I cherish all her visits with our Soph sometimes in tow
And three be there just chatting what at all we know
Our Debs a silver necklace a chalice from hence I sip
Sometimes she'll laugh out loudly and say Dad get a grip

I love my beautiful daughter always and for sure
She's an intellectual person her depth there so much more
Just one final wish I ask for her and then I'll finish prose
That she's happy in herself to date with this I'll finally close

My Daughter

Our Ali is a manager
She's the boss of all concerned
She knows the ins and outs correct
And pays you what you've earned

Our Ali is compassionate,
Caring and is fair,
But if you hush hush to her, she will question
"Who is there?"

Our Ali is a softy, her heart is never cold
She looks to me as I always did
Hey, we can't grow old!

Our Ali is a diamond, a sapphire, a precious jewel,
and I'll tell you this for nothing she ain't no one's fool

Our Ali she's a joker,
She likes to laugh a lot,
But if you catch her out a while
She'll say four cobs,
you clot!

Our Ali is a leader if certain Ilson crew,
Don't go near or injure any
My God, she'll run you through

Our Ali she's a worker,
But she's thirsty and need'th water
Our Ali is a lady true
And to one and all - my daughter

One Moment

My life lived in fragments a portion here and there
My mind looks at the people and wonder if they care
I see their auras plainly a segment dark or blue
I test the waters gently to see if all is true

Their thoughts they filter through me and rest in mind alive
I wonder at the end of all how did search survive
I feel a watcher over me a shaman maybe form
I sense a glow inside my being a feeling really warm

I need nothing or I think so but maybe someone close
Not full of words concerning a tirade there werbose
Transcending to a space unknown when I shed this mortal coil
They lay me in an oak lined box then put just neath the soil

Ashes to ashes dust to dust a man once roamed this Earth
A strong hard working villain a heart so full of worth
The words they speak endearing but lowered six feet down
A tender loving person a fool a saint a clown

Off World

U.F.Os I've seen one, or so the story goes
Is there life beyond this world out there, just who knows
Stars too many to count at all and also out of reach
With planets orbiting every one and atmosphere round each

Folk in flying saucers who travel light years to our world
Through time and space and meteors, off planets to he hurled
Books are wrote about them, people from far stars
Jule's Verne wrote worlds nor long ago
on green men from planet Mars

Time and space conundrum, what lies in the blackness there
Are stories told to children to frighten, so to scare
Plunged through the portals shaped round or like cigar
Nothing known about them, no clue to who they are

So leave the future well alone, what will be will be
And if believe in flying ships, stick around and you may see

Bonfire

Sitting in the flames of life a bonfire to be exact
Sleepers for a circle then the opening cracked
Inside the flames were roaring a tractor tyre a seat
A mite just sat waiting a sense of extreme heat
At last I burst out from its grip a flame my pals had left
I rolled upon the dewy grass my heart saddened dry bereft

My mates appeared and doubted a hospital bed for days
A mothers tears were forming I listen as she prays
Terrible scared he'll walk this plain transformed by heat and soot
From head to toe in blisters rife release from inner gut
No scars are on my body unswathed they stood and stared
My Jesus saved me on that day a spirit God who cared

Rebellion

Abused, accused and battered
From such an early age,
Filled this boy with anger,
Filled me with seething rage.

Control I knew no boundaries,
Just hate instilled my mind,
A truth I never looked for a love, I could not find
I delved into the underworld,
A crook, a con, a thief,
All saw a portrait of this man
– none looked beneath

I focused on a savagery, a brutal man to maim,
To I, it was a portal, a scene it's just a game,
Money was the object to what ends I wouldn't go,
A demon snarling, spitting in truth is all I'd show,

They asked in prison wisely
What maketh such a force,
My anger was unmentionable
But my goal was just a course,

And then one finds the answer
In later life runs free,
One learns he has a syndrome Asperger's and ADHD

Broken

Despair reigned in my spirit, in appearance I was done,
Mentally was crippled broken hearted, thoughts of gun
Emotion lay in sobbing, my life to I no more,
Physically this picture hurt, as she walked out of the door
Devastation rose before me, the roads I tried in dread
For twenty more I'd loved her, the thoughts raced round my head

Heartache through the years, as in vain I tried control
To never heal a wound which oozed, my chest one gaping hole
I ran away in hiding, for another she had sought
My feelings in my drunken state, remembered measured nought
Broken, battered, starving, I then began a search
I scoured the massive cities, through towns, in chapel church

In vain I tried to heal, my tears to always weep
The forces of my very being, bit and bit began to seep
An ending free from searching, from doubt, from inner pain
My mind in so much turmoil, a cauldron boil insane
Then my Lord my Saviour found me,
a sheep who'd strayed, was lost

I cried the tears self-pity, he said my son such cost
It took the next five years, to heal, to feel remorse
He set me on a pathway, a narrow winding course
People came to aid me, to help build my inner strength
A counsellor, a preacher man, a vision hope at length

My life this day is healing, through darkness I have rode
Now found within my being light, this is my home, abode
12/06/1999

Young Boy

That venomous speech just tumbled fortie to fill the vacant void
You treated as a worthless welp you felt aggressive so annoyed
You spat through teeth so tightly clenched, this rage I did suppress
No utterance of thoughts of peace this boy could ne'er address
You filled my mind with secrets old, ne'er could in life attempt
Then harken to this man of worth this age is non contempt

You staked my loyal heart of truth to a cross with no escapes
To cloak my being undisclosed to this world I hung my drapes
Now in my prime I peel this onion layer by layer
to unveil my precious gift
Then heal my aura of contempt to mend this chasm, rift
Just take a peek at my belittlement
with your scathing vicious tongue
Then listen to the words of truth,
in your judgements you were wrong

Inner Self

One strolls a path of innocence to look behind those eyes
To see a mass of seething hate in truth to all despise
One tries to change those circumstance to alter one by one
And yet a fleeting upset all joy and faith are gone
One adheres to save a multitude the energy strength doth sap
To look into a mind confused a barrier swirling map

Tangents we go off on to seek one inner peace
A search to take one's life span to find that golden fleece
And yet the boundaries that we set are ne'er but mortal coil
Deceive oneself and disrespect to wound with knife or foil
Just sense ones inner beauty and glance look hithered too
Then see in one's reflection the joy within is you

Paths

Two souls upon the sphere of life
What do our paths entail
For one the learning curbs of self
To experience one's jail

The other sees and so does learn
But lost between life's roads
Her spirit screams to be so loved
Yet the choices spits and goads

Two paths, one choice, is so instilled for love to who we are
No treasures deep, we worship none, no reaching for that star
We want the bare necessities; no glamour, riches wild
For in the truth of life itself, we are both just born a child

We look for justice kind and care
We ask for very little
We work through life's just hardships
We toil with scythe and sickle

Two paths entwine, not known the cause
As we meander, twist and bend
The see the truth in 'Daughter', 'Pa'
We can call of each a friend

Youth

I spied no God within my youth, just hatred all around
Amazed you'd be how far it touched, inside it would astound
Unbeknown I was dyslexic picked on in the confines of my school
To all and Sunday all around I was stupid clown or fool

Proper trod upon me, screamed temper hurled abuse
My friendship to this dying heart, I later found a ruse
Friendship this not for I, in fact I stood alone

God to I a word not seen, God was not my shield my guide
I choked the good which held my soul, then ran away to hide
My scars I nurtured unbeknown, to hone my hatred cold
A deed not I would stoop to do, no chivalry I'd hold

In I did some deeds so proud, but I could not claim refute
So in my truth darkened days, I'd say nothing deaf and mute
Picked on by the proper even God, I became an oaf and lout
In later years in wisdom given, I realise God picked me out

He choose me for compassion, I'd buried deep within
He choose me for my mercy felt, no more I felt was sin
He choose me for this massive heart that could carry heavy toils
He gave me understanding truth,
he gave me treasures gifts and spoils

Greed in former life had gone, envy greed once stood by side
Now I walk a different path, my father will never be denied
I thank the Lord for pains and scars and the terrors I have seen
For once I asked him in my heart, I was washed so pure and clean

Idealism

People ponder on reflections, just how normal one can be
They create their own utopia, envisage try to see
Two point five in children, a career in pompous tones
Then work until the life drains out the
and the creak and crack of bones

Society this symbol strong with all its faults transcribe
Human instincts nay they can't be faced all fantasies denied.
We cannot do, we do not dare, as secrets come to life
Then as the truth pores from our souls the gore inside's so rife

For when out life is but earth's dust and we conquer all our fears
The only mourner to be found is oneself mirrored tears
I state live life for who you are and transpire to earnest dreams
The find serene and peaceful calm and scribe your spirit reams

Do not look for focus in other beings their foolish sense of pride
Judge yourself in works of worth then in truth you've not denied
Masks are placed upon one forms denial, lies, deceit
We focus on the strengths of man but sway as does the wheat

We question all my options wrong do I stray and go awry
Or does society dictate our worth and strive until we die
Maybe we must face ourselves to grant ones wishes wise
To leave behind the masks of man and all the cloaks disguise

Shattered Windscreens

Can I forge ten million pieces, adhere to, stick and bind
Could I search for just lost fragments, of the shattered mirror mind
Can I piece together boyhood and the memories in place
Could I fit them all in sequence, without a crack or trace

Could the mirror hold reflection, or would the gilt be lost
Can I find the tender spaces of my thought so deep embossed
Can this mirror mind when forged as one,
can it heal this broken soul
Can it bring about a state of peace, in fact, to make one whole

Could this man who held a fairy tale, be strong and more sincere
Could he use his own experience, the charm instilled be clear
Can I make a new beginning, create one inner peace
Be on a path of tenderness, the times of past released

Could I love oneself, be open, kind, let all sundry in
Can I bring about a families scorn, bring hop and pride to kin
With help to see this inner man, this blinding flash of light
I know I can find inner peace and my future could be bright.

Will

My strength has come in handy for pick, and shovel dig
For sports, and games for leisure, to wrestle one greased pig Strength will
keep me upright in melee, fight, or battle
To keep my eyes alert of night, to quieten babies rattle

Strength will pull the birds for me as these muscles I do flex
To show my displeasure, when people hurt, perplex
Strength to drive to Norway, to heaven knows elsewhere
To help when struck a banister, as I tumble down the stair

Strength of then rebuilding, get up brush down in life
To finally get over, the break up from one's wife
Strength of will to conquer, when on the moors I trot
To become more sober as a man, instead of drunken sot

I've noticed how I've struggled, and pondered thought at length now see
how I survived it all, from inner Christian strength.

Baptism

Bathe me in thy light, Oh lord, keep me safe from sin.
This world holds many hurtful days, don't scorn my face, put grin.
Wash me in thy waters, the one of Holy Ghost.
Let me hold my faith again, to you I speak the toast.
Drape me in thy swaddling robe, care and heal my hurt.
Lift me out of turmoil, pull my face from out the dirt.

Speak to me in my dreams, Oh Lord, one whole person be.
Cloak me in thy wisdom for you the highest power.
Let me feel thy force again, give me my finest hour.
Nudge me to encourage, to tell me paths, give hints.
Carry me when no more strength like in the poem 'foot prints'.
Give unto my being the knowledge of mankind.
Let me see why glory, guide so I may find.

Wheels

The wheels of life keep turning a balance on the road
The verges made of grassy banks
some staggered home short mowed
The wheels within our universe planters static still
But comets and lark asteroids could smash out world at will

The wheels of mind keeps churning on a knowledge of three score
To find this inner peace inside on thermals we could soar
The wheels of man and woman kind to build upon such bliss
Relationships to start anew enchantment with one kiss

The wheels of oceans tidal ebb to flow upon one beach
To look upon a darkened sky the portals we could reach
The wheels rotate whatever the sanctuary thus spied
To look upon destruction girth all cascading tears we've cried

The wheels of self to overcome to feel to start a lease
To render mighty molehills flat out journey once may cease
Those wheels of mine keep turning if only people knew
That the wheels upon our family lives are attached to how we grew

Human Masks

Welcome to the world of masks – the ones we hide behind
So many I adopted, the true me never find
Welcome to the hallways of con, deceit and sly,
You ask, "how do you do it?" My answer is but "why?"

We cannot act as ourselves, we must not let others see
We pretend, when out in company, me bored, not I, not me
We put on the masks of interest, when sitting there in school;
We put on mask – not foolish – no, I be nobody's fool

We dress ourselves accordingly, not out of step, but norm
And then trot into the masses, like bees to buzz and swarm.
Our hairstyles must be trimming, not Mohican or of crew;
For to be in tidy appearance your heart must be of true

Then mask of that adoring wife with brood – the perfect mother,
But, secretly inside that mind, she dreams of yet another.
The final mask is paramount, in death with dignity die,
No kick or scream resounding, no tear-drop must I cry.

My Prayer

O lord hear my plea, open thine eyes let me truly see
Lord hear my prayer, give voice to I, so many more may share
Father give me heart, to fight for justice, on this brand new start
Father give me light, for your magnificence to shine inside so bright

My Christ give me bread, for my strength to keep,
there no evil tread
My Christ give me wine, for gentle Jesus there to always shine
O spirit give me your peace, that one day the war we won will cease
Spirit give to I your love, then in death to sail to He above

Master challenge all my thought,
to know thy grace as I now am taught
O master fill my heart with joy, heal the wounds of man and boy
Lord walk with me my mile, rest within my spirit just a little while

My Jesus hear this earthly speech, cleanse my soul I holy do beseech
My Christ take unto my will,
in your love alter mind this implore, install
Father harken to my word, except in all I've spoken,
this I pray concurred.

Optimism

I'm going to die tomorrow, tomorrow I'm going to die
I don't know what the cause will be or the reason why
I've thought for such a long time of diseases, and such like
Flu jabs I have taken, done exercise on bike

The diet I survive on, no calories or fat
I walk a distance daily, as long as it's flat
Them hills they take my breath away surely, it's not cigs
And beer I don't drink a lot a couple down in swigs

I wonder how I will go, from heart attack, or stroke
Or get knocked down outside my house, by some drunken bloke
I could fall down a pit me thinks, or maybe railway track
Or burn within a blazing fire, could roast within haystack

But no matter what I go with, I know it's them my time
And it's the only thing in life, they say dying is no crime
I'll calculate the outcome, sit down to do some sums
Hey hang about I am a fool, tomorrow never comes

27/12/1998

Decisions

Look upon your beauty not outer but inner true to self
Take care to rove a truthful path disregard a tack of stealth
A peace lies in your being a tranquil state of mind
A love is in your aura generous mild and kind
Ones folly lies in others to trust but let you down
The guts behind the facts a thief a con a clown

Take care to guard your peaceful state it shatters as of glass
The hurt doth roam your peaceful state it does so amass
Your better than you think of self let go that damaging curse
Put by a purpose true to you as of coins put into purse
Noe look upon your aura sense the mountain dew
Take pride of your successes in truth the pride is you

Hopes

No matter how one says it, its gone its lost its done
One can visualise a future on a lottery to be won
A chauffer driven transport a holiday round the world
A comfy bed and silken sheets snug and warm so curled
One's family would benefit maybe all a financial gain
Surgery for suffering folk release from agony pain

Some pennies for the bank account riches beyond ones dreams
One watches eagerly Saturday night for balls
one picks then screams
We've won we've won oh golly gee our good luck charm
Deserved by all through life's uphills a feeling calm and warm

Found

I found cigarettes a comfort, a dummy from a child
I found in drink a blessing to develop, be so wild
The drugs I found so mellow, from heroin to coke
It started with the cannabis, just a little smoke

I found that hate protected, so no-one could get near
I found certain pleasure in the people's eyes, to fear
The coppers found me difficult, to catch, to understand
I found that thieving paid the bills, plus money in my hand

I found to be a menace, a drunkard, and a fool
To swagger in a public place, with shades to look so cool
I found a shot gun threatening, a club, or knife to stab
I found the women ready, with all this gift of gab

The life took but one turning, in trouble once again
A voice within my starving mind, question, am I sane
The final stage was sickening, with my face upon the ground
Once my friend, yes I was lost, but in the Lord I'm found

Now I walk a path of honesty, my head is lifted high
To feel within my being, the flow of tears to cry
I've found in comfort sleepful nights, to do in life I can
I've found in friendship warming, in woman, and of man
I've found in Lord my talents, I'll praise, and never cease
For my Christ gives joy, and love to I, and always inner peace

25/09/1998

Cometh

Let go my child of human hurt
Let these fears to I
In faith much more than worship see
Release a time to cry
Let go the hates of bitterness
That hardening heart to me

Come let me now unshackle thee
Take cataracts to see
Let go all you despise my child
Break down the wall's defence
It's time of newer meanings
To give, to recompense

Let go harsh words to neighbour
Give thanks that you were born
Look out these eyes now given
To see a structured dawn

Let go to I your heartaches
Your peace as well as smile
Walk path I off planned for you
Walk now this Christian mile

Let go manipulation
You cannot change the crowd
The offer praise and worship
Declare this out loud

Let go your understanding of
How life should predict
Admit control you have none
But I, in you, have picked

Let go amassed the knowledge learned
In life to wonder why
For shortly you will come to see
Then surely come to I

Inside Out

Perimeters a boundary a block to human race
A binary code a subject a link to inner space
A sphere one just logs into a void just out of time
A poem or a computer puts some words that also rhyme

A book one reads to analyse a picture forms to mind
The crush its meaning sideways under hammer scythe to grind
Unsure of all the meanings to sense down to tree's roots
A hawk spies prey descending an owl just gives two hoots

One wishes to be capable to seek an inner space
The wish is outlandish the limits human race
Why does I try connection to a source they cannot see
To solve enigma wisely but then its cowly me

God created earth and life and yet created God
I study bible daily its in there but how odd
He's light of light and dark of dark a duality exists in time
Perfection to the highest realm no other so sublime

Windows

Welcome to my windows the portals to my mind
Come see through glass of clarity come see what one may find
The mass of nerves and sequences a picture book of life
The roads and paths we've strolled upon three kids and loving wife

A home we called our castle to protect from all outside
To form a love unending beauty friend a guide
But loss would throw in turmoil to destroy a past once bought
To find a mentor not of earth a God a Jesus sought

He gave me love and peace of heart he showed that life was worthwhile
Not of drugs or money grab but an aura glowing style
I thank my Father, Jesus son and Spirit to grant me peace
Bow down to praise and worship thee for my nightmares now to cease

2013

Away

Welcome to the hell pits of remand homes and such like
Try to transform it this boy this youth this tyke
A reprobate a ne're do well authority would state
Transformed they made a difference to turn insides to hate
Compassion never visualised just compulsion to its height
Tears flowed endless torrents from a child a man a mite

I couldn't show no weakness I had to be so strong
Looking back upon my life right now in truth yes I was wrong
It could have been so different if showed guidance instead of cruel
Some disciple accepted not beaten scorned gave gruel
But governments enact these laws bring justice to the mob
But never see their efforts good and they never hear one sob

Injustice

Let go this path you've taken
The one of dire sin
Ask now my child forgiveness
As peace, I will come in

Let go the shroud of darkness
Deceit, let this fly by
The come to sense the light I've given
Your time will come to I

Let this pain injustice
Bring to bear your soul
Realise the conquest,
That love will make you whole

Let go the pride and prejudice
Let the judgement make
Do not assume of others
Their way, their earthly quake

Let go those condemnations
Bring faith this gap to span
A joy in heart to see the world
Embrace your fellow man

Let go my child the final dread
The final breathe a sigh
For now, you come to golden fleece
For now you come to I

Worm Holes

It spreads itself so evenly yet we let ourself disrupt
We neigh at truth condescending add murk we stir corrupt
We seek out friendship true and good in one just to believe
And yet we turn our backs away the tongues do wag and weave

If not the truth we'll make it up condemn spill lies deceit
We'll smile at innocence in thee and appearance smart and neat
We cannot let this love grow wild we must stun thee very worth
Do not allow ones heart enrapt shackled to this earth

The mind we'll lose our very souls as we plan and pledge and plead
We'll shout to no one, let none near and so none small tarry heed
We can dance a merry dance of hope alone inside ourself
Bore into beauty once we found fill our greed with envy stealth

We'll challenge hope and charity we'll spite and slay ones pride
I'll wait in here and watch my friend for my hatreds not denied
I'll channel into unknown realms of a mind where not one knows
In there I'll feed desires of death an time as life wind blows

Just Lord

My Lord I ask forgiveness for my traits to alter hence
I know my sins forgiven I need to pay no recompense
My Father why do you bother with a fool is solely me
I don't read your scriptures daily in words I cannot see
Spoke I can hear it but mistrust the words of man

I wonder what you planned for me cos you know me very well
I falter in my earthly tasks and to know I canna spell
I ask my Lord you guide me to show a purpose meant
I know of my misgivings as a youth it was misspent
My Jesus give me insight to a knowledge you possess
Let me bare my very soul and to you alone confess

My Lord

Accused abused and battered from such an early age,
Filled this boy with anger no trust so full of rage.
The boy became a teenager a tempest storm to quell,
He sought a path of vengeance to give them living hell.

None would conquer yet again none would near his heart,
He'd become a man not nourished, all fragments drawn apart.
A villain they would shout at he a reprobate a thief,
They saw a heart of iron none could spy beneath.

And yet he wanted freedom a sense of pure release,
He begged could someone help him he queried is there peace.
He found a church but wary who abides this holy place,
He found that none there judged him, solely found sense of grace.

This man of nearly fifty gave heart and soul in trust,
No more ferrous metal heart no more pitted rust.
I praise this Lord for mercy for faith and hap in he,
And always praise my Lord in prayer for saving wanton me.
25/01/09

Gentle Lord

He watches from our onset and with patience there he'll wait
He sees the spite thrown inside out but ne'er does he berate
He give us choice to follow he, but does not scare condemn
He feeds our souls if we believe like nourishment from root to stem

He hears one waiting asking why he raps upon our door
He holds one close and carries mind as ones tears begin to pour
His footprints in the sands of life mark a time he once did carry
Then as the pains fades in our hearts we loiter darkness tarry

We go to Christ so filled with guilt with sin we ask to cleanse
We walk with thee we talk with thee
say our prayers and psalms amens
Then stride we do on open ground again we feel the gait
And left behind just put on hold our gentle lord will wait

He'll smile with thee in happy times and weep when one is sad
He'll tap upon your window pane
when in thought one thinks ones mad
He'll aid one on his journey to hope and dreams galore
And all he asks out pledge to self is your word is true and pure

Steps

They called after me a reprobate a ne'rdowell a thug
I strode my road regardless in pride my heels I dug
I walked a path belligerent untruths some cons and lies
I was racist to the human form to all I would despise

I didn't think the consequence the next to I unseen
In brawls I battled hatefully my senses sharp and keen
The light so entered being a kind and loving man
He guided to a realm unknown my sight a greater span

He held me in my sobbing to realise my hurt
He bathed me in the waters true taught me to be wise
The final fears subsided to Christian and Baptise
My King of Kings and Lord of all my Prince my sins dispose
I'm privileged to enhance my faith and the light within still grows

Myself

Sneaky, sneaky jab and run undermine all have some fun
Sit back watch it all unfold people hurting confused behold
Laughing crying I control pull to pieces make them whole
Make them weary leave so tired boundless pulsing I'm so wired

Give one look to all and sundry every day from Sat to Monday
Don't get close just hit and flee boy I'm scorching filled with glee
And yet it's their lives not my own no one close for me atone
I see through portal but do not spy my life is nought it's just a lie

Energetic but not for I all my spite I want to cry
Can't let close shut down can't be open wear a frown
I wish so wish that I could see then leave to all and just be me

Fear Engulfed

I've let fear engulf my being, from such an early age
Each step in life I've taken, in each to cower rage
Love lost to show no feeling, for fear of showing I
A film to watch with sorrow, but man in me no cry
The fear of fists in temper, a sign from father dear
The look into these bloodshot eyes, my very soul did fear

Fear of being foolish, to laugh at my mistakes
Fears of crossing over, in case the bough doth breaks
Fear of god ensuring, to take on righteous path
Fear of being forthright, to smile, to bear, or laugh
My chosen fear to hold up, behind this mind made wall
My fear to wander outward bound, to feel the nature call

Frightened then of shadows, to form inside my mind
Fear to let a human near, cautious fear in kind
Hate so filled my being, yet fear lay there in wait
To chance upon a meeting prize, none in fear to date
Those fears so long ago in past, today I bring this world
Fears of mother's passage born, when in warmth I was so curled

My life stepped in fear, from the moment of my birth
The thirteenth day one sunny June, I took my place on earth
Fear remembered, just a thought, when children brought to bear
The fear to show in tenderness, to love, to hold, to care
Now fear of days grow darker, my time so soon will end
Then fear I will cling onto, in death no heal or mend

Will fear then starve in after life, where spirit will roam free
Or will the fear which raged in life, in truth will follow me

Decisions

Decisions span o'er decades from spite a toy once stole
They shape our form opinions they mould our very soul
Love and life they bond each other to state a meaning word
A partner lies aside you yet a meaning is unheard

One drifts o'er plains and sanctums to discover just the truth
Yet she only has to sit awhile to find her inner proof
Wisdom walks in her aura and yet the darkness grows
She wanders through her mind space and sanity overflows

Tried weary frazzled her footsteps lose their gait
She ponder on the outskirts in a milder peaceful state
Now stroll those portals once again look to your inner strength
Then see all wonders of thine self to spy your world at length

Speed

I'm so tired, I'm so wired, why can't I close my eyes?
Dropping speed for euphoric state, clear my mind of all the whys
Chatter with chewing bubble gum, so's not to chew my cheek,
God the come down makes me narky makes me weak.

Drop a couple of downers to let my eye lids fall,
Try to have a piss in peace when my prick is skin so small.
Must try to burn that energy to help sleepers do their job,
Listening to heart beat thumping watching views that throb.

Three days I have been up there the parties with the booze,
Drop those last five uppers, no one to care, to lose.
The state of mind is hectic but free from fear or pain,
Then same I'll take tomorrow and after that again.

Times I've taken tablets I'm no addict as you see,
I'm so tired and restless, why can't I be me?
I'm so wired and hurting let me break and weep,
I'm so tired, I'm so wired, oh God just let me sleep.

Give's a draw on reefer man, I need to feel the sweat,
My name is Jimmy Junk Head and I've not scored as yet.
Hey man, I don't mean nuthin, I just need a pull or two,
The name is Jimmy as I've said, and who the f**k are you?

Hey man I know my name do ya think I'm a smuck?
I'll tell yer I'm like a kid I just need summat on ta suck.
Just give's a smoke I promise I'll leave ya with ya smoke,
All's I want is two a three or I'll settle for a one toke.

Come on man I'm burnin', ya can see I'm losing buzz,
Whatcha think I'm in disguise and I'm the f**kin' fuzz.
Come one man I'm hurtin', step into here and see,
Look man I am crawlin', down on floor on knee.

Come on man please for me and I don't know who you are,
But the world I live inside of here it's strange, truly bizarre.
F**k it man it's over, you're not my bestest friend,
When we attended infant's school
you said you'd be there until the end…

Needs

A woman's needs are many fold, here I'll itemise a few
A walk with hands clasped holding, to stroll the morning dew
A touch to say to I love you, then fondle locks of hair
A tender kiss upon her cheek, to say you really care

To take her not for granted, but bloom, and card do send
To be there with all troubles, her tears to dry attend
A snuggle not for bedroom, but anywhere to choose
To find the feminine side of self, else partnership to lose

To be just her companion, lover, counsellor, friend
In illness make the coffees or wounds to bathe, to tend
To wash her hair in bathtub, to dry, or towel her back
Then caress, and cuddle passion, but gently no bruise of black

Whisper words assuring, encourage in all proclaim
No falsehood in your manner, always beautify her name
Keep touching, holding, taking, give your heart of true
The says the words with meaning, my bride I do love you
06/04/1998

Transgressions

To ogle at a beauty with thoughts of yes I could
To look inside at honesty married but I would
To steal of moral status to harness wealth threw theft
Could lead to ones undoing no feelings there bereft

To battle with the mind set maim to hurt another form
May leave you in that darkened place not shelter from the storm
To use and so be selfish deceitful to the core
Your transgressions in the afterlife must cascade and outward pour

To step into the light is hard let all oneself be seen
He'll take you as the way you are wash down and make you clean
Kneel down and ask forgiveness
for the path you once walked strode
Then step into a shining light and live in your new abode

Father

My Lord you walketh by my side in tearful times and woe
You build my spirit day by day to enable me to grow
My saviour gave me talents to sing out to your praise
My cup it runneth over to your truth my glass I'll raise

My Jesus holds my future he also holds my hand
Unseen by many others are his footprints in the sand
He's known me as a waif and stray who disobeyed the laws
But he sees within my heart of hearts and also knows my flaws

He understands and cherishes this boy this youth this man
And maketh girth and stature to a universe to span
I look for reasons why he'd care from now to way back when
And all my thoughts lead back to thee
I thank and proudly state amen

Diverse Mind

The diversity of the human race from black to white to pink
Makes you stop to ponder, to analyse, to think
We are upon a planets ground in all our forms to date
Yet racist views are commonplace some peoples' kind berate.

We think ourselves the perfect form and jig our reel or dance
And like a peacock proud and stout, our statements jiggle, prance
Can't we see this human state of mind is complex beyond belief
These trillion, billion cells neath skin just as a coral reef.

Yet plunder all from mining's skill, we undermine to each
The voice our condemnations, hate in pulpits far we reach.
The diversity of human growth can surely show our worth
Then live for honest truth to each as we step upon this earth

Did humans build this world of green, of deserts, forest high
Then when we war among ourselves does no-one reason why?

Date A Base

Two copper coils one fibre optic words spin through email air
One asked a question poses thought does any really care
A fellow doddles acknowledged pause where do thy feelings flit
A person kind with caring heart a soul of worth true grit
What purpose does thee tiptoe pry into the soul of man
I seek romance with worldly wise a lifetime joy to span

Red roses plied upon my bed my tray of golden glit
True blossoms scattered hitherto true love to never wilt
One marriage plea two coupled minds two bodies one entwined
Two's laughter with a friend of past with bangers mushroom dined
Two children from the loins of John as to accepts his seed
Just Eva Ryan Jo and John do make this family creed

If Only

If only I could turn back years, stop, reverse the clock
If only I'd been steadfast, staid, if only solid rock
If only I did not hurt so much, if only I'd been true
If only I liked varied colour instead of just plain blue
In only folk could talk with, instead of hated in my eyes
If only I did work all day, instead of scheming and the lies

If only crime I did commit it was just of impish boy
If only I be someone else instead of folk annoy
If only can go on forever, the future we can't see
If only, yes, if only, all those years I could be me

Mates

You can count they say upon one hand those people who will count
That pleasant few who make worthwhile
from a carriage aid dismount
That breed of rock with open doors for the battered waifs and strays
Who daily listen to those woes then church knelt and prays
These folks I spare are far between you'll only spy a few
But as life's memories fade from light you are so glad you knew

You'll smile at times of helping hands and tears of woe and joy
These folk who aid assist get hurt but your emotions they'll not toy
These two I know they speak like I hey up ducks wheres ya been
I state these friends upon one hand with pride for John and Jean

Dreams

My dreams they are so colourful, intricate and bold
The messages that lie within, what do they say or hold
Falling down a mountain into a dark abyss
Never hitting any object, although sometimes a near miss

Looking at the future, they say it's de ja vu
Walking over meadows where was one, now two
Stabbing at my manhood, what does this curtail
That this is time yet to come or maybe I be male

I always wake accordingly to what was that about
Of the nightmares with the vampires
where my blood just trickles out
The colours that's inside our minds no-one on earth could paint
Especially dreams of godly worlds or the colours of a saint

Maybe dreams of lives gone by and they're so full of sin
But the very thought they are inside, and with a key locked in
March 1995

Again

It happened yesterday yet again the times it done just that
Fate or doom I just don't know or is it me the twat
Again I felt that this time it would differ from the last
And then as I slam the doors of mind that sigh that freedom gasp

Again I blame myself for this heart that's open wide
I am a man of talents few but enter walk inside
Again I feel upset for another broken heart
But look at I, I do not dare, do I deserve a start

Again I'll put my faith in Him for guidance to his goal
With wisdom sought and knowledge found
one hope to make man whole
Again I seek but will I find this man who loved and lost
Again that hurting nagging doubt upon this sane embossed

A Picture

A picture paints a thousand words to those who surely see,
But for I a picture hangs on wall no words it has for me.
Admitted it holds scenes abound from swan, a horse, a cloud,
But to me they hold no life at all just dreary in shroud.
I can touch a wall that is solid, a breast also is soft.
But looking in a picture frame if a garret I see a loft,

The Mona Lisa's portrait what's all the fuss about?
Match stick men on cobbled streets a house or cockney tout,
I can't see their worth is thousands, to me it is a scene,
It's not like talking to Aunty June at all, asking how she's been.
A walk round any gallery puts me in the foulest mood,
For to me oil is from the ground especially when crude.

A picture I'll admire of the naked female form,
Or a picture from the human mind, a hoard of wasps, a swarm.

Grandad's Promise

One whispered promise to one's kin
Of troubled times, regret and sin
One promise vowed to be sincere,
No drunken rogue of spirits, beer

One promise made to be just kind,
To leave a life of woe behind
One promise to his child of child,
Of once so young with temper wild

One promise oathed lost in one's times
To lift one's head from dirt and grime
One promise of a heart now pure,
To find a path intact so sure

One promise spoken to a babe,
Those tears of hurt to soak cascade
One promise when his time was low,
For now the wish of man to grow

One promise now be open feel,
His feelings showed to ne'er conceal
One promise meant so full of care,
For you, my child, forever there

My Dad

Dad I do so love you, respected for my time
Your son who does cherish you, will put his voice to rhyme
All my life was anger, at everyone, and each
All that tried to guide me, in fact to truly teach

Misguided in my being, I tried my own short road
Took monies from my siblings, but then in anger goad
I never listened to you, and now I know I should
You only tried to teach me right, respectable, and good

But dad right now I'm listening, to all you have to say
Let's spend more time together, let's book that holiday
Your son who now shall carry, for once you carried I
For once you gave me heart to live, and emotions for to cry

My dad I love you honest, heartfelt, and so true
My life has been in wisdom sought, yes I'm so proud of you
When our times are over, we'll stand in front of son
Then hug in each in spirit form, for this day we'll have won
God bless you dad
I love you, your son Clifford

Blessings

A song I heard some time ago, said count them one by one,
But what if they came abundantly, from folk unknown, our John.
What if I'd knelt to state a prayer, and answered all at once,
Would I stand in awe or disbelief, is so I'd be a dunce.

I prayed for separation that neither would get hurt,
I prayed we stayed in touch as friends,
not vehement knives and dirt.
I prayed for home to come along, the right place it to be
I prayed for furnishings three ply, and to feel so close to Thee.

I prayed that you would be my guide, and lend me to Thine aid
I asked for your forgiveness Lord and my open heart displayed.
I pleaded for a world of peace, goodwill to all mankind
I prayed that you would heal my pain and settle conscience mind.

I've asked a lot, my Lord to date, for the changes of my youth
Let go cigarettes, drugs and booze, also that vodka proof
I'd like to say quite openly, that I love Thee and I'll bow
In humility and joyful praise, I will do your works, somehow.
4th August 2008

Neighbours

Some neighbours can be awkward, some may moan, and groan
Your music is too loud for us, nothing stated, calms, atone
Some neighbours are deliberate, in their speech about next door
Kindly to one's faces proud, but once inside they've swore

Some neighbours never greet you, as you walk into that gate
With squeaky hinges ours so loud, its howdy do cliff mate
Some neighbours never aid you, no help will they apply
If needed, I'd not asked for, their questions are but why

Some neighbours can be spiteful, in none to truly trust
To live next door to mine in fact, it truly is a must
Some neighbours are so petty, the Jones' they must keep
Out houses are not palaces, but no dust in mountain heap

My neighbours they are diamonds, treasures beyond compare
And if in any struggles, I know that they'll be there
My neighbours hearts are wonderful, and both I call as friend
I hope to live a long, long time, next door to never end

No gardens go un watered, no washing left to drench
For I have my lovely neighbours, their titles Marg and Hench
19/07/1999

The Team

Jackie is the architect who got things off the ground
Chrissie is the sectorial but not in glass surround
NLP participant is a direction to the soul
Heidi deals with language which connects to make one whole
Jo has understandings to medicate and care
The team say just to ring us and know that we are there

A smile always a welcome a cuppa which is great
Taking ones endeavours such a feeling to elate
I thank the team for knowledge to a soul in search once lost
Give time and monies pending for to me it's just a cost
I wish the team a Christmas that's full of Xmas cheer
And hope the team continues for a prosperous New Year

One Dream

My gaze transfixed upon her form, sensuous this glow so warm
One woman for one trillion dreams, espied to love in papered reams
I stand away, but feel so close, a saddened heart in truth morose
No mention can I give to her, a fear she will discourage me

I tough he daily lightly brush, then night transpires I dream in hush
I see her aura bright surround, my being seethes when she's around
One day I may with courage stole, not to tremble with some control
To ask the question burning deep,
those anguished moments take a peep

I feel her thoughts are equal mine, to be as one, superb, divine
Her smile it touches to my soul, her being close I feel so whole
One day forth she may understand,
a future hence, to walk hand in hand
17/05/2001

My Mother

I met a woman through a man, one years ago to date
I feel she is my mother dear, so warm, superb, so great
I ask for help no questions, of why, or does not heed
One heart of gold this treasure, one certain different breed

I walk a street to twenty four. On my own just me
A smiling face, and open arms, she fills my heart with glee
Hello she says my sweetheart, come inside my pet
Put the kettle on to boil, a tea your lips to wet

You'll never be in need with me, if at all we've got
No I've never held a fortune close, but heart I have a lot
My house you are so welcome, make yourself at ease,
The dinners cooked come get it, chops, broccoli, tats, and peas

A pudding for our afters, are you sure you've had enough
And never go without again, I'm telling you I'll get rough
My mother she's a diamond, who sees a battle won
I class her as my second mum, and of course she calls me son
God bless you mum, from son Cliff xxxxxxxxx

Watery World

How peaceful these those waters still, mysterious so cold
To slip beneath the waters still, the darkness to behold
The waters shimmer as life's light, caress my inner soul
Those waters there would so erode, could soften heart of coal

Waters as I look to dream, turn turmoil tender quell
Rippling flowing rolling by, what does she sigh, do tell
This watery world majestic, far from the maddening crowd
She pulls bespelled one magnet, to cry in pain out loud

Emotions she may carry, to lap or rage in time
One poet sitting by her shores, would put such view to rhyme
Water, water flowing carry I upon your crest
Grant this one to conquer, to find, and then to rest

Water, water sing thy song, sing far across bared heath
Be my saviour, be my all. Then someday let me neath

Time

A poem or a sonnet or an ode to man time
Has to have a certain presence a balance has to rhyme
It has a flowing aptitude as the words take a shape and mould
It is a voice of reason or a story to be told
It portrays a sadness in one's heart or the teardrops in one's eyes

It leaps in bounds in happiness elation to the fore
It begs forgiveness pleads and woes a plea to very core
It shows a man once standing high then depths of deep despair
It hides so many heartaches to a being without a care
It maybe lets the essence to a wounded cold soul
It praises God Almighty to be worthy and made whole

The Weed

I cough me heart up daily, but still shove one int trap
A little leaf in paper, then a packet painted wrap
This habit is ridiculous I must give up, refrain
Then burning blood, a flaming, another lit again

Its worse than filthy heroin, and this is legal choice
No one thinks of cancer, lost lungs, lost limbs, lost voice
Addiction in my being, and one that must be broke
Cos it brings phlegm from somewhere, and all I do is chore

I walk behind when have none, to breathe in lungs, to smell
In truth the stink is awful, like the brimstone fires of hell
These stains upon my fingers, what must inside be like
In forty years of smoking, my breath can't stand a hike

I've tried in past so many, but always I would fail
Excuses flooding forward, the wife, the kids, or ale
Now I listen to the old folk, young folk all the same
To smoke gives cred, and kinships, these beliefs to me are lame

I've smoked sin I a young'un he boasts to all, he brags
But sure in truth there coffin nails, the weed, those cursed fags

Love of God

It's beyond our understanding, it is beyond belief,
Three score and ten an instant, our life to he so brief.
He created all our universe, the galaxy installed,
Yet through our pain, our misery, to grains of sane he called.

The speed of light is nothing, solar plains, or constellation,
Just one micro seconds thought, your touch formed out creations.
He made Atlantic Ocean, Pacific, land, and sky,
He sent our Lord in Jesus Christ, upon the cross to die.

He died our sins would be forgiven, past, present, future, light,
Then we to walk within his love, to rest, to give our plight.
Our reason cannot fathom, the depth of mind to see,
That all my life he's cared, so loved, and welcomed I to he.

He's carried me from onset, before my time of need,
He made the heavens, earth with joy, the lowly mountains scree,
And yet he looks upon me, to care to tend my hurt,
When bully boys of long ago, he lifted from the dirt.

He gave my mind the choices, to follow, or to sin,
But when so low I cried to he, he answered do come in.
My Lord, you are the ultimate, no one could take your place,
You're sinless, and almighty in purity, and grace.

I'll love you so eternally, but to never understand,
Your love for every living thing, at the tip of just one hand.
My mind cannot imagine of your power, or your might,
But one day I will stand before, to look upon in sight.

Your love spans all dimensions, beyond time, and inner space,
And yet your love so boundless, pours over we the human race.
Thank you, Lord. Your servant C.H. Latimer

Listen

Hear my cry, so shrill, as I talk with thee
Feel my pain, so cruel, help me just to be
Harken, listen deep to this scream echoed inside
Aid my desperation, dry the tears I've cried

Do not let all my tomorrows invade me all the same
Is life the ultimate sacrifice – a pun on words a game?
Aid me in my torment – see within my soul
Long ago mankind did this – broken, never whole

I hid behind the masks of time – laughed and played the fool
Put shades upon my bloodshot eyes – acting oh so cool
Reality was different – torment reigned within
None upon a planet cold – I could talk to friend or kin

My days grow darker, brethren – my time is but awhile
The seconds tick by rapidly – the shadows of sundial
My friends or just acquaintances – I wish you Bon Voyage
And hope you can be true to self, in reason, by and large

12th November 2000

Anew

No cons, or tricks, no deceit, or lies,
no treachery, no where's, or whys.
No sleepless nights, no wheel, or deal,
no hate, no fear, no rob, or steal.

No running scared, no mind games brought,
no guilt, no sorrow, no killing sport.
No main, no hurt, no rage, no lied,
no burn, no club, no place to hide.

Yes freedom from a fiery grave, my Christ came in, my sins forgave.
Yes honest truth, with love to share, upon the cross he hung to bear.
Yes kind so giving, filled with pride, a future saw, a dream espied.
Yes, kneel to pray to aid my walk, to feel, to sense, to share, to talk.

My Lord give thanks, from I to thee,
for your love, your strength, for sincerity.
My Jesus keep me safe from sin, but if I fail, let me enter in.
My friend goodnight, in love God bless,
the morn approach, my mind address.

Anew in faith, to walk thine path, be my guide, my hope, my staff.
This prayer but one a stranded waif,
keep me smiling, sound and safe.
Another day draws near to close,
tomorrow dawn, you'll lead who knows.
Wherever to, which ever door,
for each day dawning I love you more.
09/07/99

Once

I used to drink a gallon, or more with heavy heart;
Then I found a new way – I found a brand new start!
I used to drink that brandy proof – headstrong and hell bent;
Today, the only spirit drank is the one that's Heaven sent!

I used to drink that lager beer from "down under" and abroad;
New waters is my only vice – I drink to new accord!
I used to drink that "champers: which tickled up my nose;
Now I drink of the new wine – one which lights and grows!

I used to drink that purchase from taters or the mash;
Now I imbibe the Trinity, which humbles not so brash!
I used to drink a cocktail, or mixer, it's so called;
Now I walk a different path – the one that's marble-halled!

At Christmas, I used to drink a "toddy", mulled and slowly spiced
Today, I drink to you, Lord, and name you as my Christ!

Friends

My friend is always waiting, he's round the corner by the strand.
He offers wisdom and inner peace as he leads me by the hand.
He shows me insights of myself like I've never seen before.
He is salvation, hope, and pride, he is my living cure.

My friend he hides when folk approach, unknown, afraid, kind.
My friend gives confidence instils inside to all and sundry show.
He rides my thoughts of troubled times forgetful in the know.

My friend can guide and always does to me, my friends, this earth.
He shows himself in euphoric dreams, enhances all ones worth.
My friend has cool he'll chill u out and will never take the piss.
He's marvellous courageous bold his name is cannabis.

The Journey

A courtship is soul building, passions soaring plume
Current coursing through these veins, two beings so consume
Love making is a need fulfilled, whenever, where's there's room
Then time in two rolls into one as a flower buds, then bloom

A flush of cheeks one redness love, it is for one, but whom
This trust for two must ne'er be broke, the outcome loss pure doom
When true to each a thread be wove, a garment on loves loom
A ring just one engagement new, two rings for bride and groom

Holidays be bright, some breeze, those visits castles tomb
The battle grounds we watched in awe, the cutlass, canon boom
Now as with age we still hold true, as from our mother's womb
As life ebbs from one soul to death, the sorrow heartache gloom
09/05/01

Addiction

An addiction is a motion, a thought, a power trip
Self harm, or mutilation, a razor, cane, or whip
A drink inside, a feeling, a drug to make so cool
A fungi cillicibin, the drying of one stool

Amphetamine uplifter, a book to read all night
To love, to cosset ego, to make one feel alright
On life we feel the buzzing, like bees to form a swarm
A bed so cosy clinging, an eiderdown so warm

An addiction to an armchair, cigarette, or briar burn
The speed of roller coaster, or car in rally turn
An addition to a metal, papers, comics more
Sex in all complexity, we are addicted that's for sure
13/09/99

Future Light

I'll die this death tomorrow, or maybe yesterday
It could be in the early hours, confusion couldn't say
I've died and gone to heaven to see my master there
He showed me all up evils, to tend my wounds with care

He told me I had lost a love, forever I had killed
But time I grant great healer, a life to now rebuild
My master knows the outcome, he saw fore time of I
He gives so much compassion, no more I ask, but why

He guides me on forthcoming, to place inside of self
To look at truth shortcomings, to grant in strength, and wealth
My master shows a need in I, to be serene so calm in peace
A heartache long ago was wrenched, to give me pain,
but now shall cease

My master is not solemn, he's giving, kind and good
I eat of body weekly, then drink of heavenly blood
In her I find a love adorned, to give, to never hoard
His name so many titles, but to most he's Jesus Lord
To Mike in faith we live, God bless
05/06/1999

I Know

I did not know just who I was, or what this world had made
I know I feared so greatly, in broken spirit paid
I know I witnessed horrors, a child should never see
I did not know the depths of self, but knew I wanted me

I know we had a tyrant whose temper did so scare
I did not know the word of love, if so implanted there
I know I wanted friendship, someone fair, and true
I did not want this feeling dread, forever down so blue

I know I needed the meaning to be so moralistic
I know I wandered aimless, just a loveable rogue
Who talked an Ilson dialect ever so broad, so brogue
I know when booze had beat me, the drugs lay all around
I know my friend in you I sough, and praise one day I found

I know you lifted from the dirt, and carried I to here
I know I can live out my life, to walk beside so near
I know I have a prince to praise, one Lord, and master too
I know I have a friend to thank, and Jesus it is you
28/01/1999

Freedom

The onset of one journey, two look into minds space
Boundaries formed, rules to make as we scour this human trace
Feelings, and emotions as we look into the soul
Tormenting thoughts of long ago, to turn as blackest coal

The counsellor reflecting through ultimate this trust
She'll summarise our sessions, some months we break the crust
To look into dark shadows, open doors I'll beg, so pleas
The fear, the dread of long ago, a wound forever bleed

We are bound within one spirit, with she I feel secure
My pride for her unequalled, as the words from I will pour
She talks to I as client, I feel our souls entwined
This journey of one person, these memories outlined

I felt from first encounter, this broken man set free
To walk so hand in hand in love, o'er pasture, mountain scree
This freedom sought from shackles, this heart to beat once more
To look upon one future could, or destiny in store

My many thanks are given, to a lass who shows such care
Who leads me to a haven safe, beneath a golden stair
Released my mind to open, to cry with caring friend
To come to joy fulfilment, this beginning with an end
Thank you, Maggie, from Cliff

First Born

They say that, if a girl is born first,
It maketh man;
They say she'll be a wisely sage –
Her whole life there to span;
They said that she was beautiful –
A shining, brilliant star;
My daughter then from now in truth,
You're gorgeous, yes, you are!

They say she outspoken;
Oh dear – tut, tut, my, my;
They ever saw her angry
Or the teardrops fall to cry;
They did not hear her first word
"Dadda, Google Goo!"
They never saw her carry an egg
She thought she could moo!

They said that if she could hold her pose,
She'd succeed and would go far;
They say that if you're true to yourself.
You know just who you are;
They never saw the torch light,
Under covers aids to read;
They never saw the wounds of life
As her nose began to bleed;

May I speak, my daughter, to you
If you could see or only knew
You would know that sayings were correct
For in my girl, they are so true!

Show Me Light

Oh Lord again I wander misty world where love once roamed abide
Where once someone could calm the hate again to she denied
My Father show your light to I is this your treasure fayre
Will once again I shout, I yell is someone really there

My Jesus let me see thine face to conquer all mine spite
Give to I the wisdom sought to see through second sight
My master take my will I heed listen to my plea
Give to conscious thought I pray to understand to see

Your kingdom lays awaiting I let your power reign
But two of choice we welcome you let there be no pain
No more the cry of anguish rain no more to walk away
My father who so mighty fold give we light I pray

When all out times are finished thus our time on earth be done
Let us know the battle cries to know in mercy won
My Lord I pray I know I kneel to thee let. Your mercy shine
To stand in front on judgement day to open heart to thine

Swearing

I don't know why I swear a lot its maybe from a kid
In a gang in Ilson town its likely to outbid
Me dad he swore in temper, me mam I think just twice
But I've got to quall the urges cos it really isn't nice

I f and blind it all day long a list of swear words just
And if I canna swear at all its fuffulah water must
A miner once worked a pit and swearing was a way
Over tanoy they'd all f and blind you'd hear day by day

Nurture Group

He loves us, yes, he loves us, in health, or if we're sick
Our names are of no consequence, be of Michael, or of Mick
It could be Dawn, or Tina, Alex, Malc or Mags
Cliff, or Maureen, Ian, in riches, or in rags

He loves us all so equal, he loves us all at once
No matter of the path we've trod, or the road we did but trounce
He loves our hearts, our spirits, now he will wash us clean
From gutters, or from pulpits, its no matter what we've been

He asks that we may follow, to own him as our Lord
No force he puts upon us, it is our own accord
His statements are not fierce, he strokes, he does not bite
His treasures he will give to us, in wisdom, second sight

His love bestowed upon us, his gifts are many more
He asks I'll knock for always, but you must first open door
In servanthood we'll follow, we'll sing our praise to thee
Our hearts we give him gladly, in all he loveth we

The Moorhen Theory

The moorhen spied in difficulty, no swimming,
circles made the current swirling taking far, this torrent now obeyed
No more he fights to tread upstream, he's hurt a foot, or wing
I pry him from these waters swirl, in hat, to home I bring

Could you come down my sweetheart, the vet, in car, must go
Have faith restored she tends its needs, in fact she seems to know
A box of sawdust nest be made, let's see the wing or more she feeds, but
no he will not take, his crop be full for sure

She fills the bath to see him swim, he's poorly all can see reached then a
miracle cure at hand, one drop of Bach rescue remedy
He flies, he walks, he swims with ease, no more a crippled bird
But could I tell to all I meet, they voice, begone, absurd

We set him free, we watch afar, this bird I once espied within my hat I
brought him forth, this truth, but some say [lied]
My wife this tale could verify, but why will none believe it's a complex
web we spin in life, the wickerwork we weave

Animals if wild, or tame can tell, or plead for help
They do not need to cry in pain, a whimper, bark, or whelp
My story ends but once awhile, a true but fairy tale
Now men, and women, child, and boy help all endangered whale

We are not alone upon this earth, our cousins walk beside who are we to
question flight, to swim, or honey plied
We walk on two, they walk on four, no mock, or question why so help
them all, as they aid, we, this granted, by the by
24/02/2000

Planted

I stand upon this rock of God who chose this land for me,
Gave vision to my clouded sight, enabled me to see
I cannot trust in fellow man, my Lord he will give life.
My past be done, no more vile crime, no more in dagger and knife

I soak in his adorning light, my soul to he so clean,
He does not judge my every move,
knows my path and what I've seen

I trust my Lord who gave all in death, to free me from my sin.
Drown out cries of vicious man, to love children, hence my kin
I ask my path be guided, to be sound and solid ground,
I pray unto the cross of shame, so deep in depth profound.

My Lord I ask your guidance, my words from lips control,
To wander in your light of lights, in your truth to make me whole

When in my final days, last breath upon this torrid plain
In your realm your righteousness, your wisdom I will gain,

To sit beside your loving grace, the blessed Father, Son
The final battle that we face, in Christ already won
May 2022

A Prayer Answered

I knelt to pray in years gone by of distance once so small
To be so near to heart strung song to be near when hence you call
I knelt to pray for tenderness upon your lips a kiss
To look into your browned boy eye's my joy so filled with bliss

I knelt to pray for feelings emotions spellbound reason
I'd commit for you all sacrifice to walk in all one season
I knelt and cried but Lord above give me hand in hand
Let love's void to conquer all to bring to understand

I knelt to pray to cradle head to run rings through your hair
To mourn you, lost in all those years
to give a moments care
I've took uppers and downers paid a quid and half a crown as took
mushrooms and needles draw and prick

I've hollowed with the rest of them thinking drugs O.K. there nice
But in the end transparent I paid the sacrificial ultimate price

Blame

I can blame a thousand people for misdemeanours to the crown
I can tut at others antics makes annoyed to cause a frown
I can watched folk from my window
and state she's out there once again
I spy how others raise their brood and think that their insane

I'll condemn the doings others do core blimey look at that
I'll snigger at those passersby just look at that top hat
I'll whisper idly to my friends who do they think they are
She's nothing but a gutter slut she doesn't ever wear a bra

I'll mutter condemnation I'll judge folk free of sin
He'll try to come into my heart but I'll never let him in
I'll make know evil doing false true who gives a care
I'll curdle milk with poison talk and the waters deep I'll stir
I'll cause havoc with my mocking words

fill my life with lies and stealth.
Pretend that righteous fills my being but I'll never look at self.

Hurt

The first cut is the deepest or so the saying goes
The misery and heartache so lost in here who knows
The challenge is to breathe each day gain courage but a task
To plead to any entity but let me die is all I ask

To trudge each day unwilling to open eyelids why
To feel the hurt such agony then teardrops form to cry
Let me end my days with drink or drugs anyone or both
I cannot trek much further and this my final oath

I do not want the wisdom of years alone just I
To always beg the question to always wonder why
My path has been a lifetime to wander endless days
A Christian or a reprobate to see the truth who says

We cannot turn the clock reverse so anger doth replace
The demons rise within ones soul no human hurt no trace
Do not let them enter your heart make hard as mighty bone
Make cold your feelings hence to die one beating heart of stone

Love Light Future

Let your light explode inside my being, let it stretch to end of globe
Let us see our Jesus Master in your makeshift tattered robe
Let mankind see all your power to make the world so clean
Your churches father emptying they want you near be seen

Our battles with the people who are starting none belief
If you could show your mighty presence once
then all would find relief
Give us the strength to do your will both
and choose wisely to their cause
We need no vile emotion hence no threats of all out wars

The mighty men have fallen the women much the same
We trust in you my Saviour in any there's no shame
Give presence to your form refined a blessing the show of you
Then all this world so crumbling can see all faith is true

Your light can guide a billion stars a human morsel grant
Let all the nations heal this earth it's time for all replant
With love and faith His wisdom given to meet him face to face
His footsteps where He carried you do not fall from heavenly grace

Statements

Statements come in many ways from a bank or passer by
A bill for electric or gas toss aside and breathe a sigh
Last chance saloon a red one no payments final choice
In dock one stands berated a magistrate's harsh voice

A letter from the NHS an appointment waiting there
We'll consider all your options to show we really care
A note passed in classrooms to cheat at maths or more
Adding up a total there's ten and then there's score

We worry but why should we we're here another day
There's one thing that's for certain there's death and debts to pay
But we took a breath this morning put our feet upon the floor
Opened eyes so widely stand up see what's in store

They cannot chop your hands off nay that's of olden times
And if you make a song up or put a verse to rhyme
Come on don't be disheartened it's a refuge for the poor
Stand up dust down pull up your socks it's just another chore

Just You

Do not pull yourself to pieces those around you can do that
Me I act the imbecile an ape or just a prat
When you look into a mirror tell yourself a beauty there
Hold your head up always what they chant don't give a care

Put on your togs dress to thrill no matter style accord
When stressed just state a comment a sigh ah yes I'm bored
Treat yourself accordingly buy a precious gift
Give praise to self as always, your steps will have a lift

Make sure you get your beauty sleep bag eyes don't go so well
Head up push them shoulders high puff out your chest to swell
Don wardrobe that of comfort not uneasy in one's gait
A slow but steady march to beat keep those arms so straight

Be polite as always good morning and how are you
No rush a tone just listen a brush of hair to woo
So keep your chin up always not any wants a scowl
Be like a feline padding but never on the prowl

Something

Something must have happened
To crush a love so dear
And yet it is not talked about
Perhaps one sided it would appear

Something deep down inside was smashed in awe destruct
Then surely it can be built, a heart to reconstruct
Something as a word just said or a motion to dismiss
To tell a story loathing to throw a smite abyss

A challenge thrown as gauntlet up to the bearer's name
Words can do such damage and yet it's called a game
Something snapped within this being pain wracked to the core
Talk so selfish meaning the height as eagles soar

Something's been forgotten a friendship once instilled
Now it's just a memory watered down and so distilled
Something surely can be done to recompense one's plight
Bring forth some form of justice a caning with such bite

Something always something the others in the wrong
And now just silent melodies
No more I'll hear that song

Shut Down

Close off all emotions those that deal with love
Don't bring your sadness pity up your arse the dark do shove
Make your breast of iron steel none penetrate inside
Let your senses hold the key let your instincts be your guide

If they enter so much damage and enter by your will
Should have listened but did not hark again well be sunk be still
Keep one eye open whilst one sleeps they do attack by night
Not shadows in the corners there those that fill with frights

Make haste and run the gauntlet do not falter in your gait
Stand still for but a moment the daggers there await
Close down my friend forthcoming I'll not let you enter in
The choice is mine and mine only show pity hence you win

My stature is stand tall indeed be one better man
My wish to be so steadfast the rest of life my span
Too many hurts are scarred within too many there behold
And now the chapters ended my story has been told

Illness

As Gorra a code you know
Me nose dripping all the time
No coff as yet well meaning
Itching up all sorts of grime

Dunna ache and that's a blessing a comfort in old age
I'll do another crossword
Then of course I'll ton the page
Ah can speak reit when want to for chuff sake it's enough
But with this code it tekin
Ode me voice it's sounding gruff

As long as I can get about
Do me shopping proud as punch
Then what to have for brekkie
Or a sirloin for me lunch

They say don't feed a code
Ya know or a fever get confused
Mind lose so many days
And years in fact I'm quite bemused

Me nose is dripping got to
Stop and gerra tissue soft
And look at plate just
Eaten nowt there it's all bin scoffed
It makes me tired all the time a bed all snug and warm

Close them peepers soundly
And the gunge will always form
I'll get over it wi in a few days a bright spark then I'll be
A laugh out loud, a chirpy voice I be alright you'll see

Judged

You carry with you always the darkness you ensued
To harness all its power there your adhered forever glued
Your savagery a statement to never question why
You'll tote with you the depths of sin until the day you die

One thinks he's been forgiven then why such heavy load
You sought for profit daily your dairy but a code
The punishment force coming on the mount your judgement day
How can you state some goodness what ere a life you'll say

Endeavours I have travelled through storms a living hell
To while away my thoughts of past it's only I the story tell
Misgivings yes so many losses beyond belief
A heart so cold yes all would say but none saw underneath

My precious time is looming three score and ten gone by
Soon I'll lay upon the ground a groan or moan a sigh
My master in your grace I hope that you will enter mind
To see and so establish that once I was so kind

Your judgement I will take as truth a light as what you are
Then hopefully we'll play awhile bouncing on a star
Your magnitude doth hold no bounds you're real a shining beam
We live our lives as mortals
But in your grace were there to gleam

Inevitable

The end of life is coming and this we cannot stop
No corners can we see around for one vein to suddenly pop
A slate from off a building tall to penetrate the head
To suffocate in plastic bag your lungs to fill so bled

A crash in car or under bus so many ways to die
The people who are lift to mourn teardrops form they cry
Our time is one existence to achieve whatever age
A tabloid paper cutting you're on another page

Man made could be the cause of death destruction of our world
Atomic or just nuclear a comet spiralling hurled
Devastation of tornado a river flooding wild
A breeze enormous magnitude a hurricane just mild

An earthquake there just underfoot plates to move a crust
A manmade water store a concrete hole to bust
No control of any outcome to stroll awhile a bit
But face the music when it comes the bullet makes the fit

Visions

A ne'er-do-well, a reprobate, all and sundry there would shout
A violent man with vicious tones a layabout or lout
The cages they all look the same from cell or prison bars
A thieving git a pilferer stealing goods and sometimes cars

No guilt or shame lay on my brow whatever there I took
Don't harass me or put me down don't give me that dirty look
Embarrassed I'd no feeling but didn't know the cause
When telling of Cliff's stories, I sometimes got applause

I found I'd got an ailment a problem of the mind
Things didn't fire in sequence in truth no thought was blind
No facial features I discern so fights erupted more
Beaten I'd come back again
A weapon to even score

Autism my problem dyslexic in fact inside
the spectrum of many or of each
I want to see some people who guided on a path
No longer was I there again I could even have a laugh
I thank those people kindly for endeavours it has paid
This foundation for a miracle upon my soul so laid

My belief was not in I know more but a presence higher might
No beatings or harsh tones just pleasing to my sight
I found my Lord and Saviour my faith on heart embossed
From lonely days as child and waif a boy who once was lost

I sing in glory praises my king my inner light
My father master lamb of God this vision lives so bright
When one day I know we'll meet a world of untold grace
You'll hold me as your son in kind and then to know my place
Amen

Return

There's no returning from death's back door
ones mortal coil demise
Your buried with your plaque in place a sentence here one lies
No more to trudge the paths of pain the heartache open sore
No habits formed so long ago and yet we wanted more

Eye's closed deceased no envy a casket carried sung
Put under sod a statement read then earth on top is flung
A shadow there that was not I a shadow must have a form
One body toting in one's life a pulse a body warm

A mortuary slab you lay upon one does not feel the cold
And life's demise no choosing one it's a fate of young and old
One can't be careful through ones' path outlaid before you're born
No matter decades prominent too He above a yawn

They'll celebrate a knee's up a wake for kith and kin
To face your judgement ready to look closely at ones sin
Don't be scared disgruntled you'll go then lie in wait
And whatever one did die of it's always been one's fate

Hence

You knew my name before my birth and carried most my life
You stood beside when so ashamed a bloodied carried knife
You dried my tears of pity when all was gone so lost
I walked a path of hatred wrath a line was always crossed

You gave me a peace acknowledged me taught a vengeful youth
You showed me signs in visions a dream like state was proof
Your gaze would never falter I turned away but why
You held inside emotions hurt allowed this waif to cry

Broken vows you always heard my manner was of self
No happiness would reign my being a fountain full of stealth
You knew of my endeavours this man who tried so hard
Who would not let you enter in his spirit he would guard

You gave me life abundance for I to recompense
I stand in front and state my name you bought me up to hence
I cannot find the words to thank for always you was there
Your love bestowed upon this man a tribute I shall share

Auras

The presence which surrounds one can be varied differed shade
The instinct just inside the mind a life path to upgrade
The colours make a vision of magnitude of worth
A prince or peasant worthy a king or lowly serf

The picture can be darkened a vengeful spirit form
A tempest or a hurricane, one's brewing up a storm
Envy all can be espied the wander green with greed
Your aura is a demon saint whichever one you feed

Your growth is in your stance alone a gentle pleasant breeze
Kind hearted with such feeling there doth put one at ones' ease
The portal that we make ourselves to visit inner soul
The purpose of your length of life to achieve that inner goal

Many colours form a rainbow but auras are the same
Do tread with caution always some play a different game
One builds their auras day by day from just a little child
Mine a Gemini at heart so patient and wild

Transition

Being born with two identities I Gemini in fact
To look into a mirror form the image always cracked
Broken into these pieces I often wondered me
One person was convicted and the other was set free

Two sides would mean person an identical indeed
One half was quiet quelled the other a violent breed
I and I walk hand in hand, the devil and a saint
Whichever you make contact one picture would I paint

Though life has been a struggle one establishes guilt
The other dark as evil form would shove a knife to the hilt
Both sides must live in harmony or try to get along
One would do the pleasantries the other cruel so wrong

One bound in sense of grieving the other f**k it off
Walk down the street with head held high all to scorn and scoff
My balance is routine at best to see which will appear
If lucky you'll find the gentle soul if toother run oh dear

But listen I am old and frail my fighting days be done
I look inside o'er my years and always think who won

Evil

Could you see behind those cold dark eyes
to see the evil there within
A second sense a fortitude but disguise where does one begin
I know I've got a dark part which lies so deep inside
And when my anger turns to wrath to destroy is not denied

But monster more that I out there your strength you must not hide
Give wisdom to your children fold when violent do not chide
Keeping safe from harmful folk an instinct born and bred
Acknowledge all around oneself keeps you safe what's in your head

I taught my kids defensive tools to cause once struck such pain
The perpetrator of an act would no longer rise again
Your vigilance a guidance to follow all one's life
Learn to defend as always see use weapons club or knife

Your life is sacred to yourself but others all around
Harmful ways of criminals so many would astound
Keep sight of power laid inside to move a standing truck
Never fear of your predicament and always have good luck

Entitlement

I'm entitled to the dole I get I don't feel like doing work
Need to Toke my joint all day I'm lazy jobs I'll shirk
The boozer it's there looming a pint or five who cares
Talk to folk on way to home and climb the golden stairs

I find a field to lay in so nobody can control
A lane I walk so pleasant it's just a little stroll
I need me housing paid for and all the drugs I Toke
I can't go near a building they dunna let you smoke

All rights have gone don't let me breath canna do owt reit
I'm going to the pictures and prob be out all night
Now don't look at me staringly to talk about all day
Don't give me tasks I dunna want just want to go my way

So I'm entitled to me monies don't give a flying toss
So do your whispering sniggers and chat your daily goss
Now oft to bed maybe all day long a lay in that's for sure
Hey look at me old China am down on luck so poor

Illegal

Drugs you can't escape them in your face enforced
A tablet here a little toke a drink wherever sourced
Legal over counter tip are cigs and bottles of booze
They go together nicely and whatever one you choose

A snorting powder daily to keep one on ones toes
Where does the drugs all come from who cares and so who knows
We chase the dragon demon which quells our angry mind
We toke the canny in a joint a teenth to just unwind

We snort the coke to raise ones game to know and so transfix
Go out of town a country road out there just in the sticks
Amounts are seized but still they come a mountain of pure hash
Poching a liquor so distilled all ones needs a little mash

High alcohol served daily to one day you will find
The tremors in one's hands distract and it also makes one blind
But legal or illegal who cares what they all say
Thank God I found an outlet as I kneel at night to pray

Indifference

We laugh at little accidents a broken limb or worse
Get angry at a remark one's made get narked and very terse
We snigger there quite openly at disappointment ones disgrace
Then hurriedly walk down a path in one's times a differed pace

We scowl at our embarrassments a reddened face so puce
We ponder over outcomes at length what we deduce
We chuckle in a corner and never look at choice
We mumble our apologies and never hear our voice

We cannot judge ourselves oh no we must never 'ere do that
So sees oneself upstanding not a worm or little prat
We're not common in the sense of words outcomes to outlay
The traps be set by one and all our victim here our prey

Divulge nay never keep cards so close to chest
Don't go a wander at ones call to they at their behest
We want the best for only one myself just me and I
The outcomes all the same thou knows how can you so deny

Battles

A battle in the mind to start whatever source or doubt
Achieve a victory here and there but a life to live throughout
The scorn of some people's put on you the taking of one's sight
Just rumours without consequence just vermin causing blight

The battles of oneself are harsh a testimony trail
Your girth and stature paramount so go out and give it style
A battle can be won or lost upon a single word
Make sure you listen sharply do not say you haven't heard

Take notes into your mind safe keep to keep the fiends at bay
Keep closed ones mouth now muttering until a statement say
You'll hear their chorus victory but keep your sturdy staff
Your wins will come so numerous in words you've won last laugh

Make haste don't tally waiting round be bold and quicken stride
The crest of waves you'll feel the breeze the waters you will ride
So do not doubt yourself and worth do not pull oneself to bits
And think of all and sundry as worthless little gifts

Lies

They make up stories constantly to gain in others their trust
Do not speak of one's wrongdoing the heartache fear or lust
They try to cover up their flaws from feeble to so curt
Establish presence with one's poise but never feel the hurt

They say life is forgiving yet none can see their path
To convince of all ones honesty to giggle chat a laugh
They recognise their scruples as long as they do gain
Do not look at tears unfolding do not harness hurt or pain

Walk on goodbye forever more my spirit doth not lie
Why such a rift so called my friend but never once asked why
The bond be broken by some words a stab at tender heart
Now you look despairingly as our paths are drawn apart

Let vengeance be your cry for fill slay the beast ahead
They shy into obscurity in darkness fear and dread
My honesty then shall prevail my word and so my bond
To walk my path of fathers, grace a universe beyond

Memories

I think about the old days a woman and three kids
The excitement there at Christmas time opening up tin lids
A cardboard box a plaything a bus so all can drive
The holidays of camping a pitch when we arrive

The laughter and the promises all trinkets love adorn
A wedding thus there matrimony two rings and words are sworn
The learning of each other's needs desires thus so reached
A chapel or a church ensued the pastor always preached

Sundays was for dinnertime a roast with lovely veg
Raiding all allotments just peering o'er the hedge
Running laughing joking a wondrous time for all
The years passed by so quickly just heading for that fall

Torn into the heartache to roam in the darkest despair
Running sideways headlong a stop in place but where
A head so bound in shackles the blood to carry pump
The alcohol to drown the pain the ground in sight loud thump

I miss the old times really and often gaze and smile
The memories of early years a presence for a while

Faith

My faith as brought me through a lot especially in youth
I've stood before an audience and yes I'm living proof
Don't get me wrong the doubts were there but also a loving voice
To gentle whisper to this thug, it's always been your choice

The critics they all doubted me to give up drink and drugs
Then go into a restaurant and the drunks are there such mugs
I've talked to folk about my past misdeeds are many fold
Not the nicest person once a heart so black so cold

I've lived with Christ for thirty years and yes the road was hard
My sentences from early age a gamble on one card
My Lord He lifted high one day to show my altered ways
The light which shone upon my soul would last me all my days

No fear of death my soul set free to hold my father's hand
To look upon creations store one glance would be so grand
Do not wail upon my passing put a smile upon your face
Envisage me and masters call to live in His good grace

Prayers

My prayers are very varied to family and friends
Take in of people's worries my ears to trust to lend
I pray for healing others but at time forget oneself
To see my prayers are answered and the children full of health

My prayers are talking openly to a father in whom I believe
He does not put out hatred or ones fury to boil and seethe
He generous in giving those needs his light to bask
Just clasp your hands together all one does is gentle ask

My prayer list is substantial but also to the point
I ask for there no fortunes or for me to He anoint
I ask forgiveness for my past His reply it's all forgave
But self does not forgive so quick my soul in I to save

My works are not important I must walk and do not judge
To speak in mindless meaning and to never hold a grudge
My Lord knows all my flaws from birth or before that further hence
One day to see He's magnitude and my reason no pretence

I Ask

My prayers are of my family my children always first
I ask for their wellbeing and that they'll never hunger thirst
I ask for joy abounding to fill their hearts with glee
I ask for their forgiveness in the destruction of mum and me

I ask for others always my family friends and all
Not insufficient banter but for all a honest call
My prayers are to my father His son and Holy Ghost
I raise my tea in morning light to the trinity I toast

My prayers are not of common tone although He knows my voice
His will be done I hope and pray and always it's my choice
I ask for all and sundry for a world to heal with strength
And still, we gouge into our earth take all there is at length

Our waters so polluted it's all of man's own doing
The fish diminished in all ponds the silence birds doth cooing
Our master yes can heal all wrongs to alter time and when
To watch destruction all we do its' beaten yet again

Plague

The cover ups are numerous the closing of one's ports
To let a virus spread so wild it's a dilemma for the courts
Portrayals of insignificance the total death rates rise
We're done it's over all forgot then up it springs surprise

The choking cough the phlegm filled lungs a tremor here and there
The fevers rise and fall so cold my body does not care
Sweat is pouring out all pores the gagging feeling sick
My muscles ache all over my mind is solid brick

No reason in my brain except my taste of something vile
The government make statements hark we'll cure it in a while
The toilet looms 8 times before my weight is dropping fast
Is death around the corner there how much longer can I last

How many days and nights have passed in total many more
I anger at my lack of strength a taste is but a lure
My energy has long since passed I lay in bed and prayer
I hope and pray I isolate so to others I do not share

Plight

It's my story in a nutshell a word old fashioned it's my plight
At school if ere I got there in a corner dunce not bright
The hidings I'd received at home or school the scorn and scold
Made tough remarks a plenty a villain made three-fold

Canings beatings hardship wherever I was sent
Some days or weeks or even years the learning there well spent
A mockery of man or beast I stood the stead of time
A dullard without wit or sense he puts his words to rhyme

Feeling pain in different forms makes heart as cold as stone
The years have flown so rapidly at yet I near atone
I've battled harsh the discipline to lose a treasured wife
Then felt the pains intensity more hurt than any knife

The bruises heal the cuts forgot but never cuts so deep
I look back when a happy bloke it always makes me weep
I've gone from villain dunce and clown to be a better man
And live my life in peaceful realms if ever if I can

Upbringing

Our youth was tough in many ways go hungry now and then
We'd go out picking owt and nowt or thieve a chucky hen
Snare nets for a rabbit stew or a bit of bread and lard
Inside the house was bitter cold on windows iced with shard

Bread and jam a luxury for Sunday tea all week
Go to school for your milk a treasure trove to seek
Our mothers bless them all worked fingers to the bone
Outside a stone to sharpen knives a cutting side to hone

Baking bread in oven fire we'd black it once a year
Could not afford much polish shoes but children she did rear
Six of us so many mouths but water filled you up
Bread and milk me mam called pobs harken hear them sup

A meat and tatta pie be made wi gravy poured on top
Good old days with all respect a pity it had to stop
We'd laugh in later years grown up of olden times galore
But truth be told like Oliver please sir is there some more

My Path

I'm glad he's walked beside me in my strides lonely guilt
Been when so impatient a troubled youth with hate
I'm glad He waited for me instead to leave behind
I know He wanted only that the spirit I would find

My path has been hard going from such an early age
A dunce at school a fool outside no wisdom words of sage
But lifted from depravity to become one mortal soul
To find my life so cull of light in my strength was my control

All I need was to ask Him in to enter open door
To know of my existence and to understand for sure
As a Christian the path was narrow a rogue is all I knew
He took my place ne'er be seen in His presence there I grew

I started with the easy parts do not judge and so condemn
But to reach the sky with His hand upon a tree trunk stem
A better person has walked free from demons I know are real
To some upon the golden plain in fact they do appeal

But keep think eyes upon Jesus and the works He's done to say
The life of everyday is yours we live the from His choice
To survive the obliterations and sing high his praises voice

He's not forgotten each of us we were but a grain of sand
To merge together make a shape to fight for rights of land
We know we'd probably fail at most but one comes shining through
In fact my dears we've set up have a land of beauty true

My Granddaughter

Our Soph she's got the money stacks more that God Himself
She hoards it in her cupboard large upstairs and on her shelf
I save for her for college funds for books and pencils needs
Whatever I can do for her with the hopes she flies, succeeds

Our Soph has got her talents from all her family tree
She don't barter like all others the pennies off that's me
We know she's got the noggin her brains are stored upstairs
She cleanses all her precious goods and displays her trophies wares

She's been loved from such a tiny mite to become a woman strong
In all our eyes accepted she canna do owt wrong
Andy says the sun shines out from a portal in her rear
She'll say to him ah blow it out a trump that is, oh dear

She's got the wisdom and the brains to do whate'r she likes
Can go a-camping hitherto in cars or roaming hikes
We know in time she'll marry and have children of her own
We know that she will guide them safe
and their truth we'll see be shown

Portrayal

You portray yourself not guilty but inside you know the truth
You'll hide behind the shadows dark a snob you'll stand aloof
Your face a grin or laughter hence but inside you feel the hurt
The one that you accuse belittle him so curt

You'll shape a mob intimidate to forge your seething smirk
Your mind a pit of hatred, your brain has gone berserk
You draw close to you once hated berated them at length
Now your scorn and envy you'll use to gain some strength

One day you'll see the truth undone to fathom all your lies
Then harken to the roaring hordes and taste their bitter cries
You'll wave as though in friendship but nothing but a sneer
Hello good morning sunshine whenever close so near

Your spite will be undoing to your heart and spirit too
The pitch you stand in daily will gradually stick like glue
So convey your statements angrily to bitter spite and tong
But remember final judgement your voice will be your own

Birth

The birth of my three children was the greatest pride to date
I wanted what I asked a boy two girls can't wait
I walked with them and talked with them no matter there was shy
I held them close as always with broken hearts did cry

I felt I brought them up just right and not to follow me
Gave guidance what I felt was right enabled them to see
I bathed them and we giggled on rides at Blackpool pier
We watched this country high and low even Belper with its weir

On walk's I'd carry shoulder high to see the old windmill
Seek treasures from a trash or down manner the landfill
Yeah, I think we all are pikers from me mum of days of old
A pocket picked some cash in hand whatever ere we sold

All the three have traits of I but the senses aren't a blight
The bond we have the strength untold we hold each other tight
My love goes to them always I think when gone still will
We talk so honest joke and laugh talk even of road kill

My joy will never alter their faces are perfect
And never will I turn my back or their welfare to neglect
My three would fight each other but always stand their ground
The wisdom I picked up all there in truth it would astound

Their loving and their giving to any worthwhile cause
And do so without thinking in life its but a pause
We jibe each other constantly but I's fun and we are fond
I'll tell you now for certain none will break our bond

COVID 19

It's all a scam so many says a tissue for your nose
The virus deadly spreads around in bodies swarms and grows
We can't predict a cure for or if we only can
The death there so rises three score and ten may span

Get all of your injections reactions take with ease
The blood clots formed injections wrong suffer lots now sneeze
To kill off elder generations but no it's done us all
Police will knock upon your door it's pride before a fall

Now seek advice by phone that's all no face to face diagnose
And still new strains mutate in air and bodies still it grows
A death of child that no one cared poured salt down throat for food
The government so sorry but it's covid ascribe allude

Revolution that's the way make people stand and stare
Apportion blame forthcoming to challenge all that's fair
We need to make our statements for just and worthy cause
Then stand in adulation and thanks to all applause

We need our sights set firmly to anger and succeed
To quell all those who make the germs on peoples they are freed
The death toll mounts so daily it's just another path
I say where is the justice there's none don't make me laugh

Pain

He races blood a pounding
Where is it he must seek but
Alli s lost so cruel is time
His favour gone so bleak

In truth she loved another man
His note destroyed as she, but
Left along with memories of
The life so filled with glee

Do not pride yourself with
Destiny or a path true love
So deep, my friend I state
From choice of I you will
gather what you reap

Gone down the light of inner
Soul conclusions I have none
I roam a world indulgence
Including I but one

Do not look upon this written
Word and conquer all ones stealth,
Roam among the living dead for alone you'll find yourself

The Future

What's round the corner hey a life filled with happiness or grief
Turning pages of the past,
Kneeling, are you there? is there belief
Are their fairies goblins ghouls and such or gloomy clouds and mud
Would you turn back the years happy memoirs that's if one could
I'd like to think in my time that people would join hands in joy
Smiles not evil for everyone women chaps, girls and boys

Would you cure all ills of mine, would you go that extra mile
Would you give to them last tuppence a shilling or ones smile
I'd love to ask forgiveness to whom I don't know who
Is it the person sitting next to me the neighbour is it you

One thing is for certain
things come to its conclusions sometime more or less
Then a cancer hits the nerves a stroke occurs MS

Twenty First

When thou first came unto this sphere
a star was born a pulse appear
Every now and then in life
An energy emerges two people meet

And a bond, a friendship then converges
Now birthday girl must leave this realm
where bonds of souls first sought a dream
Thought prepared this day a keepsake now has been caught

Don't look back once sorrow leave
Be happy walk your path think jokes
been told and hugs so fond once smiled a chuckle laugh
Yours twenty first the date of tears when pals we'll feel along
but precious drops of salted pure for in life I've found my friend

His Realm

We'll see the light on entry a portal narrow beam
We'll visualise His magnitude and everything will gleam
The halleluiah chorus will praise from dawn till dusk
We can look back at our body left but in truth it's just a husk

No hunger pangs no thirsty throat to his manna born
No hatred there or vengeful soul none to rally scorn
We'll see His might and splendour them marvels to create
His love will hold in constant love no harshness to berate

He'll call your name to sit beside His wisdom shining through
There's trillions of all souls around and then there's only you
You'll never ask for mercy no need your sins are forgave
Just promise to be honest true and of course you will behave

He'll wander with you hand in hand and wrestle on the ground
His voice you've heard so many times but now in time profound
A trillion there glowing stars giving life to all
Be wise and true to heart and soul and wait upon His call

Cleansing

I've nearly come full circle from the innocence of birth
A family born into it's time to earn my worth
As time went by developed into a scoundrel rogue
A fashion icon not at all no shoes of style like Brogue

I sought an easy living in truth that's what I thought
But crime of any substance one day you're afore a court
Send him down a reprobate we do not like his kind
But bars held wisdom and violence instilled in brutal mind

The day released a vengeful soul sought of other crime
I've done my porridge easily no moan of doing time
Let no one near a lesson learned don't let them enter soul
Keep hearts as cold as granite keep mind as black as coal

Keep counting all the dough ones made establish fists of steel
Do not cower from a fight ensued do not weaken beg or kneel
But now am getting on a bit they call it yeah old age
So now I'm back to innocent just turn another page

Beaten

Accused abused and battered from such an early age
Filled this boy with anger so filled this man with rage
I cannot point one culprit who wantonly did beat
A father knew no better than to kick and punch mistreat

Friends were just like packs of dogs rallying for the top
A fight broke out all would join so none to ever stop
Withdrew from humankind I did no tear drop as I withdrew
Myself a loner on my own the human race was through

I'd take my wants and needs of course to quell the hungry man
So many decades flittered by in truth a lifetime span
Truth and trust did not appeal a hardened soul to grip
Drunken nights and drunken fights as booze we all did sip

My fear held me in the dark no light inside my door
A flash of hands some tears went by in fact about three score
I know my life upon this globe has not been good to date
But victim for so many years filled this heart with so much hate

Snaffle

The holiday was planned quite a while ago
The questions where's and why for the answers to and fro
Discussions going deeply into a private mind
Debs she's buying doggy treats for whatever dog to find

The laughter there is daily we always have a laugh
The house is really nice you know an interesting little gaff
Our Soph she's coming down tomorrow meet ragbags off the train
She'll sigh a bit as always and knows I'm such a pain

A piece of fish is offered snatched quicker than a gull
All meals have been so hardy and ate till all are full
Its only on our third day but up and down we trek
The birds are eyeing prospects a chip to nibble peck

Cards at night just bastard brag or nine card winning stacks
Our John throws down his bloomin cards on top of others packs
Our Sue she's winning all the loot several pounds to date
We talk in Ilson dialect is tha comin an alreit

Steve he brought some onion rings shared by one and all
Going down an incline I nearly slipped to have a fall
We've tasted each's food in truth it's been lovely such delight
The cards are making other names like thatcher but no spite

The clan is not complete ya know there's Ali and her spouse
It's such a lovely area and the lodgins one big house
I don't do any cooking it would fill me full of rage
And in truth they pamper daily bones creaking their old age

Soon we'll pick our Soph up with banners flying high
It's welcome you our ratbags she'll blush and force a sigh
We got her off the train you know I shouted ratbags here
She smiled and hugged me laughing and where's my glass of beer

Our Deb says buy a belt to keep jogs from falling down
A rude remark of swinging balls I'd look a Charlie clown
Steve is going home today cos of new life upon the way
Already said a prayer for her and parents good I pray

Chowder bloody lovely with a great pile ah mussels and all
Mushroom risotto beef chips scampi enough on tab for all
The chowder envy will be quelled at aleberts eatery
we're back today
I hope it will be all the same as nice as mine I'll pray
They've done the climbing mountains so sleepy times for all

When tea's put out on table top they shout or holler call
Come and get it afore it's cold don't moan about the share
Don't come to me wi' problems down road and see welfare
We're packing all belongings so no rush in early morning
We've reached last day and walked a lot
we've earned our bloody corn

So now it's off to Ilson proud where we can talk and be alrieight
Reminisce about our hols for months and of each we'll always bait
The suns been kind the company sound the food to all astound
But going on we've got to ease and put our feet back on the ground

No more cakes and breakfasts two no elevens like hobbits tales
We're dieting for now on in so not scared to jump ont scales
This hol was brill fantastic and ended with all a smile
So preparation sorted and thanks to all worthwhile

Memory

No photographs inside my mind I cannot picture all
Bring fortunes to fore advance the long the short the tall
My memories in tatters I sometimes all forget
It's like a sponge so full of holes or an anglers fishing net
Because I can remember things from hence a thousand years

But look have been thru mill thou knows
and ad copious loads of beers
Me brain has shrunk in time and space old age is creeping in
I even talk to me sen and ask where I have been
It's no good asking may yer know prime ministers an all
I canna stand fer very long I av ta lean agin a wall

I get confused with names and dates someone always says remind
The get lost in mindful fog drive off and leave behind
A fold they want thirty years for me it's beyond belief
All I do is park me bum chill out ah such relief

Am seventy-one can't hack it canna run uphill down dale
It's like having turned from athlete to a tortoise or a snail

Self

The past can drag you down the pitch can stick to you like glue
Your prayers to ask forgiveness the Lord will see you through
We make our beds to lie upon just like our daily lives
The contempt and hatred all inside in fact its born and thrives

We feed our demons or our saints to satisfy our need
We back into obscurity in the shadows hide our greed
We harken to the gossips talk to secrete a morsel clue
And there again the past ensues to stick to you like glue

We utter pleads unto our king in truth to make us whole
Then succumb to habits of our past in mind there's not control
We dare to think we can destroy our earth of pleasant green
The language that our tongue projects to self what does it mean

We can't look at selves adoringly so pull all others down
Myself I hide behind a fool in accord I act the clown
Our thoughts and ways are paramount it's of the human race
But wake each morn and testify to heal in God's good grace

Self-survival

I won't let any close to me to rip my heart in two
It's been done once but ne'er no more an axe had chopped in two
My pain of lost the anguish there the bottle the only way
I stumbled all the time you see just from day to day

Homeless but no begging just watched what's throw away
The in the bins a plenty just like a tom cat stray
I'd got some talent to survive a rabbit mushroom pot
That's from field our onions what is in there what's got

Nettle soup dandelion root coffee we'd shout a proper whoop
Berry picked from bushes adds flavour to the pie
We shelter with small branches bends cover sods to make it high
Our needs are in this earth called home lets roam and get a change

To listen to the chorus dawn
and unbeknown this spark for truth romance
Our realm has took a billion years to cool and form such life
Let's not destroy its magnitude with sickle spade or knife

Let's find the seeds or other plants for us to sustain grow
The fight for our piece of mind in abundance stored
and act of which know

The Cry of Life

One cries unto the world I'm born, with a strike upon one's bum
First breath is took expanding lungs, this applies to only some
Others do not make the cry still born inside the womb
The bell doth toll no gift of life in God to parents whom

Life's a treasure we should look at close
like a grain or snowflake form
The body of a human soul is like a furnace keep it warm
Feed the body and the soul but also feed ones' mind
Go out and seek one's paradise go amid all humankind

Let life and light transcend within, give host to others near
Do not walk upon this earthly plain, in doubt, in greed, or fear
He gave us breath to speak our minds to open heart and soul
He knew our path afore our birth our choice to make us whole

Give him the lead and let things be, none other can supply
In death the final victory at peace a gentle sigh
We'll meet upon His mount of love our master King and friend
Then know his truth abounding He was with you to the end

My Life

I owe my life to someone who sits on high above
He died upon the cross of shame for to grant the earth His love
He shows to me in many ways His mercy so sincere
I hold my breath in waiting that in time He will appear

I own Him for the beauty in surroundings which abound
I look into a starlit night and mother earth our ground
I know He tends His flock in truth and hope's we see our flaws
He winces at the selfishness and the venom in our claws

He only wants the best for us to cleanse our sinful thought
He's fond of manners not of hate from each were often taught
I owe my life to someone who forgave my evil way
To show my thanks there daily out loud I utter pray

My thanks are never ending from early life He's always there
My burdens which were many fold I openly hand my share
My pride of self has risen from a person heart so cold
For my master's light inside I grasp my truth is there behold

Doors

The door was closed so long ago don't look back just look to me
The path upon a distance forms is the choice which sets you free
No shackles do I chain to you no fetters holding down
You are my sons and daughters upon one's head will lay a crown

Do not look at past endeavours just follow guiding star
Your mind is but a vessel store just learn but who you are
Doors open when in readiness to pave one's portal zone
Be ready for the tests of time and the position you are prone

Let go the baggage of your past lay down at foot of cross
Then leave behind your sins of past do not crave to sow emboss
My child your strength is limitless your glory is so too
Now bathe in light just soak in me for in I the trust is true

You've risen to our paradise an endless course for you
Look out upon the mass untold with kindred spirits few
The rapture here a fortitude all manna fruits galore
You reached the kingdom of your choice because your heart is pure

Resentment

I resent those accusations so false when heart is true
To ridicule integrity which will turn the air quite blue
Your name is but a by word to throw your stone in scorn
A Christian and soul mate who states she's been reborn

Lies and tittle tattle upon the lips of life
Words can damage deeper a cut from any knife
The truth is seen in ones belief to justify a cause
There not a thought of trouble felt and done without a pause

One knows there is no guilt to hone a spirit so set free
But accusations do abound and most are aimed at me
No truth behind the allegations in truth it's all absurd
A friendship thorough ignorance a little spat of pride
But look back long and hard at thee nowhere is there to hide

Falsehoods are the enemy they rattle like a snake
The love is lost for all time the heart to now forsake

Worship

My King is not in human form His spirit's endless trail
Omnipresence in all states of life the treasure trove unveil
My Lord who gave His life to live among His people's throng
The Master of our universe praise halleluiah song

My friend He holds me close to Him through fire's bitter storm
His wish is my obeyance in His light I bathe so warm
My guide whose always fed my soul to become so close to He
I cannot think in all my years, why ever He chose me

I talk with Him quite open there is nothing He doesn't know
He's bathed my spirit hurting the pains of long ago
My prince of peace is saintly but no honour does He ask
No hardship will He punish in His light it's there to bask

My Lamb of God you died for I forgave my evil way
I asked forgiveness for my crimes knelt in church to pray
My Lord I beg eternally that you'll stand here right beside
Be my mind my soul my heart on my path to gently guide

Aftermath

The pleading tones land on deaf it's all been said before
None shall enter hall of hurt to again attack the core
My heart's been broken a thousand bits none shall do again
No more the whimpering tear drops in mind there is more pain

None shall cross the threshold to carve their name in stone
Nothing in the darkness to none I shall atone
Wrack vengeance to my being try to break strong will
Acid turned to water my spite is in there still

You act as if nought happened a slight and cruel remark
I leave you there exhausted upon another quest embark
Your tears do not concern me they are of your own accord
My feelings getting flimsy in fact I'm getting bored

The honest truth not seen by you knocking on your door
Now lost that friendship once was honed now an open sore
Your pleadings are so meaningless they lack a certain depth
Goodbye so long farewell my friend a kinship should be kept

Sorrow

One thinks true love again been found but shattered by and by
Considered not one farthing my heart hurts why oh why
Placed my trust misguided in a person with no name
To her the hearts a plaything romance is just a game

I ache the sadness looming each morn I take in air
Carry out my chores all day look around but you're not there
May I die tomorrow so this fire inside will cease
Put down my foolish notions to finally find some peace

It's no good begging do come back their love has lost its flare
Compassion just a by word in truth they do not care
Withstood the time of ages a love so deep inside
My sorrow and shortcomings my tears I cannot hide

The drink my friend in times like these to quench the pangs of pain
Then drown unto unconsciousness float with the water rain
I've tried my hand at loves bequest bound by blood and hurt
Maybe in another life I will rise from ground this dirt

Consequences

You have to live with your mistakes and bide your time to once
Learn by mistakes you've made to hence if not your called a dunce
Patch things up where ever you can show kindness to your host
Do not break your promise binding do not brag ignore or boast

Anger portrays nothing it shatters bonds of past
You'll hunger for a friendship lost you'll starve as in a fast
Do not take your words of open heart to tarry hold the bolt
Be kind and gentle love abound do not pull-on reins to jolt

Talk sense in sentence of your voice called there to chide
Make most of your surroundings clothe in modest form
In later months the chill both bite a scarf to keep one warm
Remember bonds to harness keep rekindle touch him kind
Whispers if the need is sought
no hurt to harass spare a spiteful mind

Desire is not paramount but honest feelings true
If let down by friend in tow then the end is nigh you knew
God bless sweet dreams good night take care
Remember say sweet nothings so words to each may share

Homeless

To live upon the streets of where a box for bed and board
A scrap picked up a morsel there in jacket there to horde
Paper padding on cold nights you learn from all around
You never look at faces for a penny you might have found

Soup kitchens or a bread roll have something in one's gut
A search around allotments some veg and there some huts
A little bin with chips long bought but eases hurting pangs
Get out a copper call in morn upon your shoulder bangs

To sleep in there the countryside a forest glen or field
To find some goodies all around a stick to hobble wield
Defend one's quarter against all odds no matter of their size
And then a gift a bed one night with glee a great surprise

Marching with holes in shoes socks and God knows where
A begging question often rebuked a copper can you spare
A dangerous place upon the streets as darkness stretches out
Sleep one eye open all the time keep safe there whose about

The Kid

This kid was born to poverty a second son to date
In later years he'd write his poems describing to relate
Some bread and lard for Sunday tea a luxury in fact
This did no harm to kith and kin it kept us all in tact

My Mum would bake from dusk till dawn however did she cope
A smiling kind of mothers love not one for moaning mope
She'd bake our bread in cast iron stove and scones for Sunday tea
You sought whatever you found to eat what will be will be

Tin bath in front of coal lit fire I was fifth in line
A bar of soap no lather form the water looked like brine
Dirtier when washed me down from scum for all went first
I chuckled with me Mum right there but under breath I cursed

Nee mind it brought me up in time and put me in good stance
I found my traits for all things good even found romance
My upbringing was harsh and strict and yes we had it rough
But built a spirit hard as nails hardened fists be tough

My Mum I'd look to always we had a binding bond
And although I was in trouble lots she still adored was fond
We went on hols in later years not all the time but some
To Skeg or windy Mablethorpe up north to wise and Morecombe

Yes we had our hardships and hunger sometimes great
But Mum would make up summat in fact she would create
Both are gone my Mum and Dad photos are my pride
Back then some years so long ago broke down and yes I cried

Acting

I watch the films from yester year and the acting is sublime
Today I watch and boredom starts
there a mountain they must climb
No facial their expressions it's not of life itself
A horror core not likely a mobster with no stealth

Disasters just forget it they haven't got a clue
Even in the porno film it's not even rated blue
Make new of olden film they try ten mins I switch it off
Even violence they cannot hold in olden times I'd boff

Their even trying series with whoever they think is best
A stripper you feel can't go wrong can't even get undressed
I buy DVD's a plenty and can watch them time again
A comedy which makes me laugh a sad one causing pain

Tearjerkers now there's a film a bit of sand int eyes
Who dunnit's or a scandal in all they still surprise
I keep watching hoping someday they'll make a movie fact
But please ask the old players or someone for once to act

Death

I'm going to die tomorrow don't know of what or why
It may be of a stroke or not last breath just make a sigh
Maybe it's a heart attack it's quick an over done
Might go out bit later have a drink and have some fun

Maybe I'll get knocked over you know by a double decker bus
A splat of meat upon the ground no pleading and no fuss
I could drown int bath wi bubbles cascading forth
Don't know in which country or maybe here up north

Fall off a cliff me namesake crash into seething sea
I'll die as one does always alone bye, bye just me
And when I get to pearly gates I hope Peter lets me in
I hope I've done my penance just absolved without no sin

It's no good pleading innocence He knows our every thought
I did my time an lied a lot in truth I have been caught
I've got to think this out a bit sit down and do me sums
Ang about tomorrow is today so tomorrow never comes

Hoard

My belongings scattered everywhere from telly top, to floors
If allowed I would hang my pictures on all my doors
But rules are there in writing of things one cannot ply
No questions are allowed at all no reasons to ask why

I collect of varied items from marbles to stoneware
Onyx eggs abundant when depart my family share
Some coins a few not many not really my in thing
I calculate my spaces here and in the flat I bring

There's paperweights abundant until my son said Dad
He took the lot displayed them brill all manner items had
There's dolphins tigers owls an awl most are on display
You canna get owt else in here my answer canna way

If twinkle in my eye or heart and barter for it's worth
I wudna be messen at all and lose me place ont earth
Av gotta make a profit a shilling here and there
Me pockets nearly empty but honestly don't care

Queues

I'm not too good at waiting in a line to God knows where
A meltdown inside my head I know when nostrils flare
A condition in my make up to me I'm just of norm
Just crowds bring out the worst in a blackness raging storm

Escape into a peaceful site where things are quieter hush
Confrontation is a melee zone fists flying there to crush
I cannot read expressions go troubles soon ensues
A battle ground awaiting whatever weapon's we may choose

A syndrome known as Asperger's an umbrella take
My mind a swirling whirlwind asleep or then awake
A maelstrom in my centre being a bottomless pit inside
All emotions cascading there most humans can't abide

No worries I'm a longer so stroll my daily trek
With hope's there is no trouble there or for kindred soul to wreck
I cannot stand those people who talk with hands at speed
I'm also of dyslexic form no books or leaflets read

I try to be more social but always have to pay
But at the end as always to I it's just one day

Misunderstood

Come in I say without a smile not feeling great quite low
A few words asked are you ok feel crap is all you know
Not feelings of resentment no hidden meanings there
The phone call f'ing blinding I felt you didn't care

Not true I did not feel that way no harshness in my heart
A trust's been dented terribly a drifting miles apart
Called a liar when you're not it punches to the core
And still they say I'm in the wrong fell flat upon the floor

No apology accepted cos none was given thus
Then lovey dovey phone calls forgot don't cause a fuss
But deep inside the hurt expands into a darkness glare
My life at all none believed a liar so all beware

New tactics are the realm of light but still suggests she's right
Don't want to argue cause a scene myself been up all night
It's still in there inside of me to grate and make a sore
But I'll not succumb to battering my mind shall even score

Sin

We walk our daily lives at a trot or certain pace
We ogle all and sundry this is our fall in grace
A thought can harness evil from down the very pit
We judge that's all around us on our conscious duly sit

We masquerade in dressage a prance a little jolt
When finding out our own mistakes into hiding duly bolt
Our envy for another path instead transfix on ours
We look to greater kingdom those golden looming towers

We portray a certain servitude once a week our church
Then scoff and hone our hatred as all we do besmirch
Our tolerance is nullified no honour for our quest
We seek our kingdom all at once at our own behest
We forge the fire's daily the pictures in our eyes
And preach to others soundly our portrayal full of lies

Our only hope forgiveness the Master Lord our host
Welcome in the Lamb of God our Saviour, Holy Ghost

Temptation

It will always be there with you the pangs of this your past
The comfort of a dummy sucked so now It's outcast
Smoking of the week to make a mockery of self
Cocaine to take one higher and fill your mind with stealth

Amphetamine a rushing power enabling to speed
Magic mushrooms dried throughout to multiply succeed
Whatever drug we cling to the bottle just a sip
A reefer rolled so lovingly the end to gently clip

Tobacco most is legal a fortune to be made
Then once addiction so controls the moral is obeyed
A year or more ongoing and daily do I crave
But someone close encourages come on now just behave

Our skin it crawls with anguish just one a pleading call
But take unto your drug of choice you're heading for a fall
Keep on the fight with vengeance pick up the mighty sword
Sit down and breath into pure lungs it's true you're only bored

A Liar

I was branded a liar from early on in life
Distinguished as a reprobate that's including of my wife
My parent's they knew the score my Dad would thrash some sense
But later years inside myself a kind heart to recompense

I know I was a rum un and no one round would trust
A savagery strove in my being a darkness fight and lust
Trouble always followed me with faults from sin my birth
My fate as luck would have it put on muscle there some girth

Shoulders broad and muscle worked honed to melee fight
Some thievery was rolled in one whatever in my sight
Comparing none all under my a wastage nothing chaff
As long as beer poured down my throat then smile and av a laff

My fortunes were of many fold some in prison fold
None in there was trusted ones heart of stone so cold
But all was mine own doing no other could I blame
They always ask do you regret my answer there's no shame

Pastor

A pastor from Presbyterian a Scottish man of faith
I talk with him so humbly no judgement feel so safe
He gives advice when needed and tells of poem to end my book
When finished he and lovely wife will surely take a look

We always have a smile for Jack and how's your day so far
In talking with this man of God you know just who you are
No condemnation from his lips his gift is kind and good
To church he goes with Sheena with to sip the holy blood

I speak with him in volumes another book to write
Look forward to some other poems if a word as such contrite

Worthless

Worthless yeah that's how I felt and shunned away to cry
You're not welcome in my holy place corrupt go on and die
Judge for past discrepancies not known of why or where
Just bugger off you toe rag filth get caught within a snare

No feelings do I feel for she there shattered fragments dust
My heart was open oozing blood again it's formed a crust
None will break into a trillion bits scattered to the sky
My troubled youth yes horrible but surely no need to ply

I've served my sentence with my life a future tried to aid
My path of rocks and quarried holes the bitterness and snide
Still not worthy that's how I felt do your penance more
It's not enough the years I've trudged forgiveness of three score

But walk away I will again no torment anguish doubt
I'll pull through the debris and holler scream or shout
My heart I'll guide from daggers sharp ne'er a point go near
Then thirty years in darkest mind so full of all my fears

Abandoned

I've walked away again as countless times before
No marks upon my aching heart in fact it isn't sore
I pledged this thing some years ago it saves a broken heart
And in days some other comes along wrap up a brand new start

Just leave yea that's the best way no talons holding on
She'll find another clown pretence a Michael Bob or John
No tears again cascading no pleading heartfelt moans
Cross another highway sort county coded zones

I said none here would break my will only one is up to hence
I guard my back and also front pushed hard against a fence
No crying wailing moaning it is of course her loss
She'll ring a dozen times or more in truth don't give a toss

Words cut deep you would not believe a plaster for a knife
But hurtful jibes from once such love in fact a loving wife
My path is crooked I know that my realm is where I'm fed
To lay wherever blindly as long as it's a bed

A Friend

Friendship yeah, it's ominous you can count them on one hand
They should listen to your tales of woe and say I understand
They should never judge or scorn you hold high esteem so true
A hug or cuddle gently a pat on t'back when blue

Share problems not one sided but take each other's side
A friend in need a friend indeed no need to scurry hide
But low behold it happens they let one down again
Chatter to their comrades all insults no refrain

You ask why do belittle to shoo away just go
Read mind in all acceptance as thou indeed should know
The final straw as broken a horse or camels' back
Next time they see your face again another there thrack

Forgive is in your nature let lies fly up above
Pray to father heavenly they accept His purest love
I'll walk away as always none shall come so near
The message is so simple stay well away in fear

Walk Away

My yonders are the present my past is of today
A simple gesture walking aargh yes I'll walk away
My feelings not of hatred I kneel on earth to pray
But certain as I am of stance my pang is walk away

No bitterness I hold inside no thoughts of whom to slay
My stating to another no choice but walk away
No condemnation holding on no other persons say
Ah yes, I've done so many times in hurt I walk away

I should not question rhyme or reason upon a floor to lay
My soul mate total negligence my pattern walk away
Endeavouring to keep alive a trust no amount can pay
I have to do it every time I have to walk away

No greed I need no recompense no guilt just free and gay
And so many friend the endings nigh I arose and walked away
The final beats upon my heart the piper I must pay
They'll lay me 'neath our Lord green earth my final walk away

Long Ago

Your remains don't lie in sacred ground a cemetery of choice
Your sounds of life have long since passed the chatter of your voice
No markings tell your tale of death no flowers upon a grave
None will know of how you fought so fierce yes so brave

You can hold your head up high you know none would utter stop
Some soil a meadow lane or fence a lonely there out crop
Be peaceful in your sleep of time do not awaken hence
For life is but a masquerade in truth it's all pretence

I think of you there daily and sometimes visit lone
A judge may find me innocent but in I must atone
The time has ravaged site and self now an older man
Some decades and so many years a presence one life span

Your gifted with a conscience one to feel one's guilt
But fear abounds inside oneself a whisper there will wilt
My Constance is I did a deed not nice and no respect
The grass grows higher every year a field one must neglect

You

You poured scorn contempt upon my being judged me so in depth
You wounded deeply the bond was broke insult in there crept
You spoke a thousand words
but none your silence was your tongue
You hurried out of sight and mind and never thought of wrong

You stuck as venom poured inside dissolving all our trust
You hid your love from near my sight again my heart's a crust
Your hatred sped like pellets from a smoking gun
Get out my sight and mind you cry in haste I had to run

The perfect picture postcard I thought for time was left
Now some dying petals a rose so cold bereft
You stole the goodness from me and tossed it to one side
A look condemning sideways in fact more of a snide

No verbal conflabs daily and none in future time
The love once felt so honest true has turned to greasy slime
No plasters can heal up the wound no stitches sewn in place
The words that cut the deepest all from the human race

Too Late

A note it started off with that then pleading crying roar
I don't know how it happened can you tell me I implore
No memory or scorn contempt of shoo'ing I away
No telephone good night God bless just verment go I pray

A judge you sat high power there's only one who knows
Inside my mind regretfulness for decades ebbs and flows
I trusted as a friend indeed to see but not presume
And yet you wanted monies worth my soul to now exhume

Your choice was on the opting the value of a word
You shunned away a dearest friend and now you feel absurd
Your loss my friend I've no regrets my heart I did so shield
Attack with actions verment tongue and aye to clever wield

You broke our bond of love ensued I'd let you right inside
The trust and truth exploring now your just denied
Do not cross my ever ending for you'll come off the worst
I've been through battles hardened a sip to quench my thirst

Deep

Cut deep into an oozing wound to penetrate doth hurt
Just shrug your shoulders so be it don't give a damn so curt
No remorse upon your tongue no regret of damage done
Then chatter to your family all it was a bit of fun

Now ended a good friendship a trusting equal bond
Now you'll see the darkness and whatever lies beyond
Your loss in truth you'll realise mine eyes for only you
But false you were in honesty your heart of spite not true

Now go and play your life of games and wander aimless way
Do as you wish your fortune gold come back I'll state just nay
When clarity doth clear in mind when fog is blown to dawn
You'll ask the question why did it end from me a simple yawn

I've forgot the times we had with each no more in grateful mind
The miles are in front of me and your just left behind
My heart now healed in glory my soul of purer form
No more I feel the biting cold inside I'm snug and warm

Weight

We carry weights upon our form
from the moment of your first word
Through one's life we pick a phrase a chatter verse you've heard
We tote those irons heavy on shoulders of our girth
The heavier the burden the more you think it's worth

Our troubles are of daily grind our workplace home or sleep
The baggage all forgotten now until one takes a peep
Pandora's box is opened in plain sight is all our sin
Spied in all its hatefulness how did I let them in

It's no use slamming close the lid it's naked for all to see
We try to unchain our worth but what shall come will be
Worries of our family how will they all survive
Multiplying worry more and disease will enter thrive

We make no bones of what we've done but long ago in past
But stay with you a life time's worth you stare in awe aghast
Well, well, now, now let's see your soul what colour black or blue
Now that a peek be honest what part of life is true

Judgement

One judges others all around but does not look at self
No portal door all shadows to cling the slimy stealth
I try to be judgmental but also inclusive of I
You can't condemn another being without the questions why

We modestly do our walks and tittle tattle all
Never looking at oneself inside there's nothing there so small
Regrets in life I've many but cannot reverse my time
To breath the fragrance of my youth to put my thoughts to shame

I try in true endeavour a non-judgemental man
To aid in listening to a plight assist that's if I can
But people walk so blindly and put worries on a shelf
No look inside of torment no eyes to look at self

Yes I've done wrong doings and paid the price for each
A prison is a school in fact other cons are there to teach
My crimes have been abundant to many for to share
I'll write a poem daily who reads may also care

No Fear

I will not entrust this heart of mine
for you to scorn and pour contempt
To leave a barren wasteland to subdue alone exempt
My heart and soul exposed to all my fears and dread to show
Your pins of pain are paramount the heat of hate doth glow

I'll not buckle with your sobbing tones the bonds been broken thus
Pretence that nought has happened be right there with no fuss
You might as well took hatchet and hacked at my defence
The hurt is in the here and now the pain is now of hence

No rhyme or reason was your stance to belittle so as child
But now you're feeling my contempt the other side so wild
My fury holds no boundaries the fuel from pits of hell
No future is there then for us no prediction to foretell

My honour means the world to me my grace and mercy too
But harken to the harshest words these don't apply to you
If I'd walked away from hurt before and do so yet again
No other love I'll search for now to give my heart refrain

I will not let you burden me in truth I'll not let you near
You ask come back be as before my answer sharp no fear

Build Up

The task the Lord has given you to be that guiding light
No need of strength muscle bound no melee there to fight
Your stage and path as always will be narrow under feet
Your open heart and honest soul a multitude you'll meet

Get down with them in homeless crowd's search for more
Some will be the start of life others three score and ten
Their questions brutal honesty my time you tell my when
The gift of life He gave you a power to entrust
And maybe staff of spear at some time you will thrust

No casualties lay on the ground all are filled with light
You see it in there, that blush that shine glow from God
Just whispers in one's mind just open as peapod
Save grain and see so healthy and plant this pleasant land
To look upon the fields so tilled how crop we understand

How world we'll help but as of now pollutions ravage hence
Something to drag our oceans just a common garden fence

Own Up

I've lived a thousand lifetimes with the guilt I've had to tote
Dull needles in my skin so hard upon my arms was wrote
I've defended I thought precious a family in fact
Done some many dealings sold drugs in veins a tract

My mind was filled with methods how can I wheel and deal
Found the women interesting my character appeal
Money is just paper to spend or make a call
Face the music wisely when your backs against the wall

You summon from the darkest depths a seething mass to swarm
A furnace blazing brightly inside tornado storm
A battle so ensuing the victor must be I
Then walk away your blood lust a breath or just a sigh

When asked did you so witness my answer always nay
And soon the summons hits you in a courtroom you must pay
Do one's time accordingly let your anger always burn
Inside or out a crust to make come on one has to earn

Safe

Keep a shield around one's heart of truth to keep from torn apart
They find a way to filter in right from the very start
Your armour is not of metal form it's fortitude of mind
Keep close your friends and enemies hoist they chain and also bind

Do not let them roam inside to slash all sacred so dear
Insecurity a wisdom a caution to follow close and also there to fear
Once inside they can devastate do carnage to all your meant
To those whose sent are nothing from below there really sent

Focus on the light inside let Master fight our cause
Let Him guide upon the mount to show God's holy laws
We must look to our Saviour the one to bring us forth
Maybe journey's long or short will take us far up north

We cannot see our work fulfilled but wait and state a player
We know His omnipresence so in fact He's always there
Cast your stone and baggage lay them at His feet
Do never pick them up again to your prince to finally meet

Sleep

My nightly nightmares vivid do haunt my needed sleep
Forgiven of myself some years my waking moments weep
The baggage I still carry I might to dying day
I cannot tell to anyone delude in any way

I'm trepid in my footsteps as I walk around my mind
Looking at the past of selves to see if one be kind
I've hated all my beings so brutal hard disdain
And yes, I can say moulded through harshness hate and pain

My patterns are so varied in sleep an hour or three
The maelstrom is still there in mind can't let others see
A loner in my daily life in dreams I'm always lost
And as the years just filter by the time in past such cost

A Christian yes in worship to praise and not in stealth
But as Jesus forgave me long ago it's hard to forgive oneself
In time I pray there nightly to see His shining light
To enter in His door way and feel His aura might

The Void

The emptiness inside this soul to outweigh any depth
Over countless years I've plied my crafts into feelings never creep
My outer being a prism one of many grades
My inner realm a prism made coloured different shades

A crystal ball I hold for self now must spy inside
The depths of me are secret bound a place where I can hide
No peace reigns in this darkened hall footsteps racing wild
Been there from my onset a babe adult or child

My problem is the walls I've made holding all my sin
A prison made by I alone can't get out or others in
No portal light just darkness looms swirling strong gyrate
Spitting venom angrily my words so full of hate

One day not long I beg implore they'll lay me north the sod
Many on this global plain a sigh relief thank God
No bitterness I'll hold within no hatred in my head
Fortunes lost accordingly so what I'm gone, just dead

Also available:

From Hurt to Healing
A Collection of
Thought Provoking Poetry
Compiled by Sarah Hall
and John Latimer
ISBN 978 0 86071 867 3

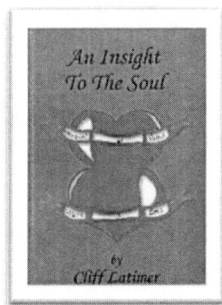

An Insight to the Soul
Cliff Latimer
ISBN 978 0 86071 858 1

Reflections
John Latimer
ISBN 978 0 86071 845 1

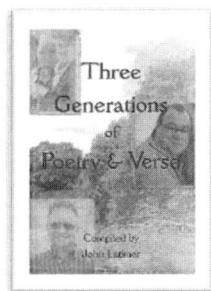

**Three Generations
of Poetry and Verse**
Cliff Latimer, John Latimer,
John Latimer (Jnr)
ISBN 978 0 86071 838 3

A Commissioned Publication Printed by

MOORLEYS
Print, Design & Publishing
info@moorleys.co.uk · www.moorleys.co.uk